George Lindsay's
An Aid to Timing
Annotated Edition by Ed Carlson

I believe that some of the points I have uncovered will go into the ultimate solution, although someone else may have to re-discover them.

George Lindsay

SeattleTA Press

ISBN-13: 978-0615720371

ISBN-10: 0615720374

There are two things that strike me about Ed Carlson and his new book. First, Ed is the defacto expert on the topic akin to Steve Nison and candlesticks. Second, the subject matter rips the skin off market analysis as it delves into muscle, nerves and bone. Carlson explores how events unfold in the market not unlike a Tom DeMark. And in a similar way, this book is not for the casual investor. If you are willing to put in the mental effort to understand what is written here, the payoff of genuine understanding about how the market moves will be priceless.

Michael Kahn, CMT, Editor Quick Takes Pro market letter,
Columnist, Barron's Online

Ed Carlson's new book on the work of George Lindsay is a must read. Actually, this is a book that you don't read, this is a book that you study. Lindsay introduced some of the more innovative cycle work in the annals of cycle research. Lindsay was a rather controversial figure but was highly respected by his peers.

Larry Pesavento, Author, Trader

Ed Carlson has, in this fine book, rescued from the dusty archives of Technical Market Analysis, the important work of one of the early masters of the craft, George Lindsay. In the age of computer drawn charts, instant indices and lightning-fast trading the principles put forth by Lindsay are as applicable today as they were a lifetime ago. Carlson has preserved the actual words and examples of Lindsay's but has, with his annotations, brought back to life principles that are basic to markets and that must be understood for all who want to know how markets move. This book is a must read for all serious students of all trading markets.

Richard Arms, Arms Advisory

Cycle analysis is still a quite under-represented technique in technical analysis. With this book Ed Carlson opens a virtually forgotten treasure in this field. George Lindsay was one of THE pioneers in the field of cycle analysis and his work can be truly described as ground breaking. Ed has made the extraordinary contribution of describing the complex techniques of Lindsay in an intuitive and practicable way. This book is a MUST read for everyone who believes that the financial markets, economies and, indeed, the entire world are driven by a fascinating natural phenomenon – Cycles!!

Michael Riesner, Head, Technical Analysis - UBS Investment Bank

Ed Carlson's last book, *George Lindsay and the Art of Technical Analysis*, was our *Stock Trader's Almanac 2012* " Best Investment Book of the Year". George Lindsay is surely one of the stock market's all-time greats as the discoverer of his famous "Three Peaks and a Domed House" pattern. In this latest opus Carlson delves even deeper into the realm of Lindsay's market timing and analysis methodology and once again masterfully brings these unique and amazingly accurate techniques to the palm of your hands. Read and understand Lindsay's market interpretations and you automatically become a superior investor or trader.

Yale Hirsch, creator of the Stock Trader's Almanac

Acknowledgements

My sincere thanks to Sam Hale for sharing the only copy of *An Aid to Timing* that I have ever found.

Contents

Forward

I had previously read "Selected Articles by the Late George Lindsay" published by Investors Intelligence. Among those articles is one titled <u>Counts from the Middle Section</u>. Attesting to Lindsay's genius, I quote what he wrote relating to his discoveries: "How is it that such very long-term counts prove accurate to the very day, or close to it? As we all know to our sorrow, the market is made up of a succession of advances and declines of widely varying duration. No two of them seem to be of exactly the same length. My theory is that, unequal as they are, they always come out even in the end. Such seems to be the nature of price movements."

In reading Carlson's book I was impressed with Lindsay's emphasis on forecasting the EXACT times of market highs and lows. In my market letter of April 12, 2012 I pointed to that mysterious point of inflection when a stock reflects the pull of market gravity. Question: Why does a stock stop going up at a particular moment of time, its point of inflection, the point when the stock is mysteriously being called home? I quickly summed up that market truth: A stock records its point of inflection when it reflects the rays of the general market and the pull of gravity. There is no news. It apparently occurs by divine design. In this book, Carlson shares how Lindsay was able to discern that divine design.

Joseph Granville

Introduction

"The first original idea I ever had on the stock market remains the best. In 1950, I published a copyrighted pamphlet 'An Aid to Timing' which introduced the concept of the 'Middle Section.' In all the years since then I have mentioned the principle only once in my advisory letter. Counts from the Middle Section are my prize way of calculating time in the market."

– George Lindsay

In 1950, while living in Los Angeles, California, George Lindsay published his seminal work *"An Aid to Timing"*. Lindsay had migrated from New York City, with his mother Nellie, to join younger brother Frank in Los Angeles to work at the Douglas aircraft plant during World War II. In 1945, at the end of hostilities, George, along with 100,000 other employees, was laid off from Douglas. It is thought that he spent the next five years working on his market timing theories as he was unemployed from then until he started his advisory service in 1951. But the late 1940s were surely not the only time he spent developing his methods. Lindsay had owned a seat on the Chicago Board of Trade from 1939-1940. He had probably been developing many of his ideas while working as a commercial artist for Macy's during the 1930s while in New York City.

Sixty-one years later, in August 2011, FT Press published my book *"George Lindsay and the Art of Technical Analysis"*. While researching the book I came across several references to *"An Aid to Timing"* but was unsuccessful in finding a copy. It wasn't until after that book was published that Sam Hale sent me a sheaf of old Lindsay newsletters which he had kept in a file for decades. In among those papers was a copy of the mysterious, missing document. *An Aid to Timing* is a paper (Lindsay referred to it, alternatively, as a brochure or pamphlet) explaining Lindsay's Counts from the Middle Section model. His monograph takes the 1983 paper of the same subject to an entirely new depth. Most importantly the paper explains Lindsay's Long Cycle. The Long Cycle provides the framework for Lindsay's methods. An explanation is found nowhere else in the Lindsay corpus. The difficulty in obtaining a copy of Lindsay's paper illustrates the importance of preserving this critical piece of work as it is quickly disappearing. Rather than re-write the paper in my own words I have chosen to publish it, in its entirety, in this book. I have divided the paper into three chapters and annotated it with my own comments. Lindsay's writing style can be difficult to read, assumes the reader is acquainted with topics not covered, and is a product of the writing style of sixty years ago. It is my hope that my annotations will help the reader to better understand the paper.

I still remember my first semester in Business school when, on the first day of class, my macro-economics professor began the course by admonishing the group of M.B.A. students that we should not expect a passing grade through a regurgitation of facts on exams. In order to pass his class, students would be required to obtain a true understanding of economics and, in order to reach that level of "understanding", we would be required to 'roll up our sleeves and get our hands dirty'. That enjoinder comes back to me now, decades later, whenever I consider what is required to understand the work of George Lindsay. Reading about Lindsay's methods is a necessary requirement to an understanding of Lindsay, but it is not sufficient. To learn Lindsay requires that one roll up their sleeves and get their hands dirty with experience. Reconstructing Lindsay's models and charts, as well as practice creating one's own charts, is crucial. Similar to a musical instrument, the student will never learn to play the piano by just reading about it. Those students and analysts who dash from one new indicator to another in search of the "sugar-high" of finding something new will find Lindsay's work a slog. Those who commit to a true understanding of his work will get the fulfillment which others only dream of as the total theory unfolds via an understanding of each individual model. The understanding obtained as the process unfolds can only be described as wisdom. As one moves through the Lindsay corpus, he is guaranteed a number of "ah-ha" moments when the proverbial light-bulb comes on. That understanding even transcends the markets as Lindsay showed in his 1969 book *"The Other History"* (Vantage Press, 1969, out of print). But that is beyond the scope of this book.

Since the Enlightenment, philosophers, scientists, and mathematicians have been trying to explain natural phenomena using mathematics. What we (other than physicists) seem to have given up during the last 300 years is identifying the phenomena itself. Our rush to atomize and explain our environment has seen a corresponding, slow erosion of the awe ancient man felt in his observance of natural phenomena. Lindsay's time intervals are that phenomena. Some people in our modern age of linear-thinking find Lindsay's concepts difficult to assimilate. It is better to think of Lindsay's models as a series of overlays similar to a crossword puzzle. This book does not attempt to explain the phenomena but to share it. To show "how" it works, rather than debate "why".

Taking this idea of "natural phenomena" one step further (and away from the work of Lindsay), note the repeated appearances of dates throughout Lindsay's work which should ring a bell with modern readers (i.e. December 7th, September 11th, etc.). Spring and summer solstice dates are well-represented as well. Many of the dates included here correspond with full and new moons.

Lindsay passed away in 1987 after more than 25years of writing newsletters and, unfortunately, without ever writing a book on his market timing methods. Consequently, this book and my previous work are the result of my cobbling together his old newsletters and piecing together his approach. It has been an endeavor which could not have happened without the kindness of strangers. The fact that these people have held onto these old newsletters for decades is a testament to

Lindsay. He was honored, in the early 1980s, with two appearances on the national television program <u>Wall Street Week with Louis Rukeyser</u>. In 1991, in recognition of the outstanding contributions he made to the field of technical analysis, the Market Technician's Association posthumously bestowed its Annual Award upon George Lindsay. Those contributions have lain dormant and largely unknown until now.

Chapter One

Chapters one through three contain Lindsay's original paper *"An Aid to Timing"* and my annotations. Chapter one includes the basics of identifying a middle section and foreshadows some of the concepts presented in chapters two and three. Lindsay's original paper showed, in great detail, how to identify the important points within the middle section (turning points and measuring points) but he didn't provide charts showing how the forecasts played out. Rather, he simply listed the dates in the four tables he included. I have added charts which show both the points he identified in the text of the paper as well as additional charts showing how these middle sections played out in forecasting highs and lows in the future.

Chapter one explains, and provides examples, of both ascending and descending middle sections. It then shows several examples and explains his method of counting. The middle sections shown prior to the tables are all based on the basic cycle (explained in chapter two). The final examples in chapter one (after the tables) focus on major middle sections. These middle sections are larger than the middle sections based on the basic cycle as they are superimposed over more than one basic cycle.

Understanding the difference between a basic cycle and the basic movements will prevent confusion due to the similarity of terms. If not already familiar with basic movements, it is best to read chapter five prior to chapters one through three.

As you read through the first three chapters you will notice Lindsay makes references to specific page numbers. Those page numbers don't correspond to this book so I have included references adjacent to his own.

Chapter Two

Chapter two includes Lindsay's concepts of the long-cycle and the basic and multiple cycles that make up each long cycle. It is not known whether he had already developed his concept of basic advances and declines (together with their standard time spans) by the time he published this paper or whether basic cycles were a forerunner of the concept of the basic movements. Regardless, it is easier to grasp the meaning of basic cycles if one has an acquaintance with the basic movements. Basic movements are referred to throughout this chapter and reviewed in chapter five.

This chapter contains Lindsay's explanation of how to count to a limited number of, but very specific, highs and lows in the long cycle. The advantage of knowing where to expect these particular highs and lows is that they show how to overlay the basic cycles and, in turn, from where to count the basic movements. Despite the small number of specific rules, middle sections can be used to count to a variety of turning points in the market.

Tables three and four show several examples of major middle sections and how they forecast highs and lows. These "major" middle sections are longer than those illustrated in chapter one as they stretch beyond the time span of a simple basic advance or decline. It is suggested that the reader spend some time becoming familiar with the final three long cycles in Figure 2.1 before starting this chapter. They are easy to remember and familiarity will reduce the need for constant referral to the chart.

In this chapter Lindsay also introduces the major cycle. This concept can be very confusing as the definition Lindsay provides is cursory. In my own experience, I have found it best not to think of it as a cycle at all, but to regard it as only the end of a forecast by a large middle section.

Chapter Three

The final pages of Lindsay's paper comprise chapter three. In it Lindsay presents a plethora of examples. These examples illustrate how to match middle sections from the basic cycle with those of the major cycle in order to forecast major market inflection points. It also makes clear why an understanding of the basic movements is more than an academic exercise. The chapter assumes the reader has mastered the terminology presented previously in chapters one and two.

Chapter Four

Chapter four is separate material from "*An Aid to Timing*" and focuses on a different, but related, subject. This chapter describes Lindsay's approach to both identifying the important 15year interval and forecasting the intensity of the eventual decline which always follows it. Identifying the 15year interval need not be as involved as the method explained in this chapter. Lindsay had written that the 15year interval can stretch from "any important low" and, hopefully, that is not a concept which requires a computer algorithm. Rather, common sense is what is required. However, for forecasting the intensity of the correction (following the 15year interval) this method is invaluable and one of Lindsay's simpler models. Unfortunately, no similar explanation has been found concerning market lows following the 12year interval.

I found this approach in a two-part technical supplement to his regular newsletter titled: The Long-Term Intervals Ending at a High dated May 14 and June 16, 1964. It also turned up in his speaking notes for presentations given to the Society for Recurring Events on October 14, 1970 and the Technical Investment Club of New York on October 19, 1970.

Chapter Five

For those readers not already acquainted with the long-term intervals and basic movements, explanations have been provided in chapter five. Students will, in all probability, find it necessary to read and digest this material before a complete understanding of an *"Aid to Timing"* is possible. For those readers already acquainted with these concepts this chapter will better serve as a review and reference section.

The majority of turning points (but not all) in the middle section counts shown by Lindsay in tables one through four are either basic highs or basic lows. An understanding of basic movements and their standard time spans is important but should not require extensive study. The chapter also includes a variety of various principles and concepts which are important to an understanding of the total Lindsay methodology but do not play the same integral role in *An Aid to Timing* as the long-term and medium-term intervals.

Chapter Six

Chapter six is a case study of the 1950s and begins where Lindsay left off in *An Aid to Timing*. Throughout this chapter the question of whether the long cycle ended in 1942 or 1949 is addressed. The reader should find the case study of great help in clarifying and solidifying much of what is written in chapters one through three.

All charts in this book, other than the Typical Schemes, are of the Dow Jones Industrial Average and were created in MetaStock©. Other than the generic Typical Schemes, Lindsay did not include any actual price charts in his paper.

An Aid to Timing

Chapter 1

Ed Carlson

1. An Aid to Timing

A method of measuring the time and duration of price trends will be outlined in the following pages.

Although the underlying principle operates in many time series, it will be applied only to stock averages. The early record follows the indices of W.B. Smith, A.H. Cole and Edwin Frickey, which appear in "Fluctuations in American Business 1795-1860." A daily index from 1861 to 1884 has been computed for the purpose of the study. The Dow-Jones and New York Times averages cover the recent periods.

> In his +25 years of newsletters Lindsay's work only covered equities. It is of great interest, therefore, that he writes here that this model can be used "in many time series".

THE TURNING POINT

One method of calculation will be used throughout. It is an arithmetic count of the exact number of calendar days. The count is started at an already established turning point.

Two factors are always necessary to establish a turning point. First, it is the moment when the price touches the highest or the lowest level in a period of time. Second, a count from some previous turning point must expire within a few days of it. The intra-day high or low is used, not the closing price. In the Typical Schemes, the turning points are represented by the letters A and J.

Important: Lindsay used calendar days, not trading days, and intraday highs and lows, not necessarily closing highs and lows.

When Lindsay writes that *"a count from some previous turning point must expire within a few days of it"* he means a middle section in the basic cycle must match the forecast of another middle section taken from the major cycle. This idea is developed as the paper progresses. He also writes of "chains" of connected middle sections.

Turning points, A and J, can be thought of as "localized" highs and lows. See Figures 1.2 and 1.4.

LOCATION OF MEASURING POINTS

The number of calendar days is counted backward from the turning point to a date still farther in the past. This point exists only in relation to an extensive movement which is called the middle section of the advance.

The requirements of a middle section are two distinct declines. Both declines must occur during the same uptrend. One of them,

Market action between points B and H is referred to as a Middle Section (see Figures 1.2 and 1.4).

Essentially, a middle section is a pause in a bull market during which the advance slows down (an ascending middle section) or when a bull market experiences an outright decline (a descending middle section). When the rallies fail to exceed point B, it is called a descending middle section (see Figure 1.2). When the rallies in a middle section exceed point B, it is called an ascending middle section (see Figure 1.4).

usually the second, is the deepest reaction in the advance. Although there may be a net gain or loss during a middle section, the essential concept is a broad trading range between two periods of sharply rising prices. It is shown from B to H in the Typical Schemes.

Reactions are the pullbacks in the market, both before and after the middle section, which act as book-ends highlighting the middle section. A middle section is defined by two reactions which interrupt the uptrend. These declines, or reactions, are the declines from point B to point D and from point G to point H.

One requirement of a middle section is that the rate of gain (the slope) of the advance must slow between the reactions; the market must advance less than it did between points A and B and between points H and J.

The analyst counts backwards from a turning point to a measuring point found in a middle section.

The number of days between these two points is the number of days to be counted forward (an "equidistance") from the turning point to forecast another turning point in the market; i.e. a tradable high or low.

Measuring points are points E and C.

Turning points are points J and A.

In the rise of 1914-1916 [Figure 1.1], the middle section began on December 27, 1915. The first reaction continued until January 31, 1916. The second reaction extended from March 16 to April 22, 1916. Several rallies intervened between the two declines. None of them equaled the price level of December 1915, before the first reaction began. The middle section was therefore of the descending type, as illustrated in Typical Scheme 1 [Figure 1.2].

> In this example of a descending middle section, Lindsay obviously thought it important to point out the two "reactions". The student will ultimately want to focus his attention on the two rallies (the final rally in this example ended on March 16, 1916) which occurred between the two reactions.
>
> This example is a good illustration of Lindsay's description of a descending middle section: "a down trend in a long bull market interrupted by two rallies at roughly the same level".
>
> Side note: December 27 to January 31 is 35 days. The distance between March 16 and April 22 is an almost identical period of 37 days.

Figure 1.1   *1915-1916 Descending Middle Section*

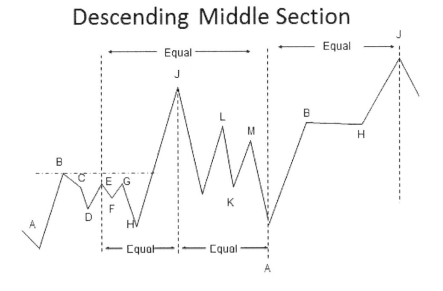

Figure 1.2   *Typical Scheme 1, Descending Middle Section*

In the 1944-1946 advance, the middle section started with the decline from March 7 to 26, 1945. The second reaction was from June 27 to July 27. The rallies between the two reactions surpassed the high of March 7, before the first decline began. The middle section was therefore of the ascending type, as shown in Typical Scheme 2 [Figure 1.4].

In an ascending middle section we want to identify the highs of the final rally (G), the next-to-last rally (F), and the second-to-last rally (E). Lindsay refers to the next-to-last and second-to-last rallies as the 'final rally but one' and the 'final rally but two'.

The only requirement is that the three rallies be clearly demarcated from one another.

The last decline of an ascending middle section (from G to H) can become a descending middle section in its own right and is typically longer than the reaction following point F.

The same basic advance can contain two middle sections that are entirely unrelated to each other.

In this example March 7 is point B and June 27 is point G.

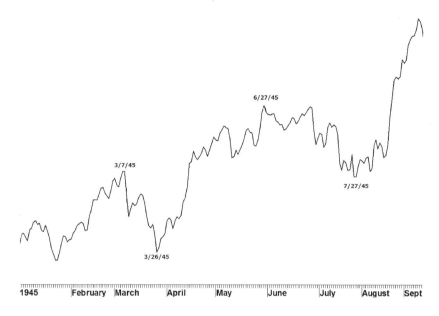

Figure 1.3   *1944 Ascending Middle Section*

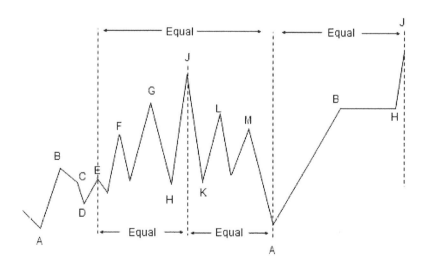

Figure 1.4   *Typical Scheme 2, Ascending Middle Section*

An entire middle section is most easily recognized on a weekly chart. There are two measuring points in every middle section. In the Typical Schemes, they are represented by the letters C and E. They must be selected from the daily record.

> Measuring points are points E and C. See Figures 1.2 and 1.4.

Point C always falls in the first reaction of a middle section. It is the first day on which the loss is approximately as great as on any subsequent day in the same downtrend. But it need not be as severe as a selling climax. Examples have been: September 21, 1897; July 8, 1901; December 7, 1904; June 9, 1922; November 22, 1935; September 25, 1941; March 8, 1945; and March 7, 1947.

> Point C is easier to identify once point B is understood. Point B is the high point of a minor topping formation. This minor top is found at the top, or beginning, of the first reaction (bookend) of the middle section.
>
> The topping formation may go on for a week or two. Point C is the day the market falls cleanly under the low of the minor top formation. The "*first really weak day after a top*".

Figure 1.5   *Point C, September 21, 1897*

Figure 1.6   *Point C, July 8, 1901*

Figure 1.7   *Point C, December 7, 1904*

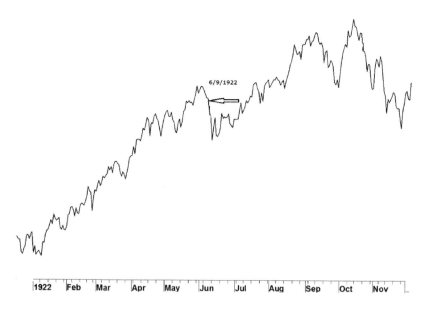

Figure 1.8   *Point C, June 9, 1922*

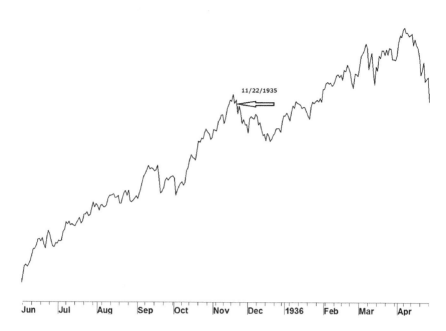

Figure 1.9   *Point C, November 22, 1935*

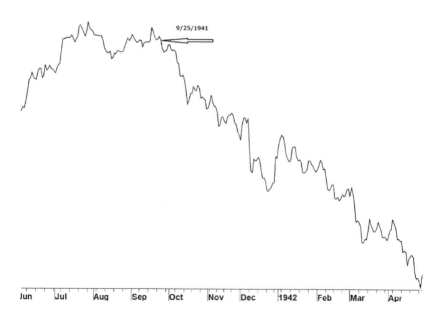

Figure 1.10   *Point C, September 25, 1941*

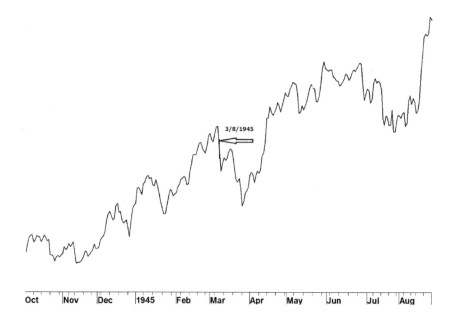

Figure 1.11   *Point C, March 8, 1945*

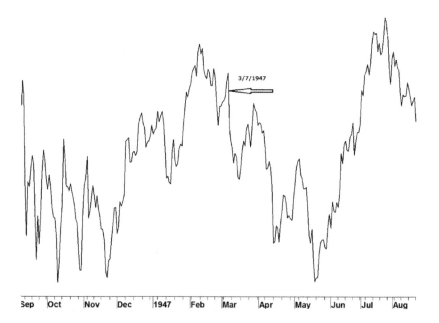

Figure 1.12   *Point C, March 7, 1947*

If the high before the first reaction was a multiple top, a point C may follow any or all of the peaks. A middle section began at the highs of October 18, and November 3 and 19, 1910. Point C could have been October 24, November 9 or 28. When point C precedes the last peak of a multiple top, the loss that day need be only moderate.

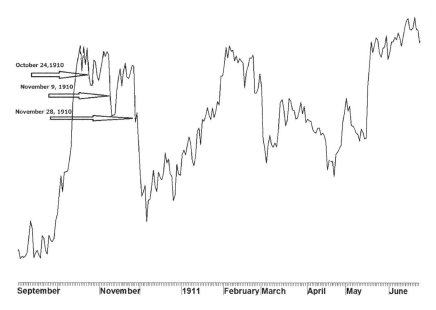

Figure 1.13 *Multiple Points C, 1910*

There are always at least two rallies between the reactions that define a middle section, and there may be more. They must be identified and counted. Their duration is proportionate to the length of the whole formation. In short middle sections, the day to day fluctuations constitute the rallies.

Typically, we think of a descending middle section as having two rallies. In an ascending middle section, while potentially having more than three rallies, we are only concerned with the final three.

When the decline from G to H contains two rallies at about the same price level, it becomes a descending middle section.

In long middle sections, a complete uptrend counts as one rally. All the sell-offs which separate rallies in the same middle section should be nearly equal in extent of loss. No decline that occurs during the course of a rally may be as deep as a sell-off which separates any two rallies. In most cases, it is merely a question of counting the only rallies available. They stand out on a chart.

Point E is always a top day in one of the rallies. If there are several peak days separated by dips, point E may be any of them, regardless of whether it is lower or higher than the

In the early to mid-twentieth century, the word "line" was used to designate what technicians today typically refer to as a consolidation. A period of time spent fluctuating around a common price level.

others. As a rule of thumb, the highest day is considered point E. But when the top of the rally forms a line, the last of the daily peaks within the line becomes E.

The rallies are counted backward, starting with the last. In a descending middle section, the last rally is that clearly defined rally which precedes the main part of the second reaction. It may be higher or lower than the other rallies. In all descending middle sections, point E is the last rally but one. The middle section of 1916 [Figure 1.14a] had two rallies of about equal amplitude. The last was from March 2 to 16. The last rally but one was from February 1 to 10. Point E was the high day of the penultimate rally, February 10, 1916.

> Translation:
>
> Point E was the high...
>
>   ...of the next-to-last rally...
>
>   ...in the descending middle section.

Figure 1.14a   *1915-1916 Descending Middle Section*

Figure 1.14b   *1916 Descending Middle Section*

In Figure 1.14b, point E on February 10, 1916 counts 679 days to the bear market low on December 20, 1917. Counting an equidistance forward into the future forecasts a high on October 30, 1919. The bull market top was four days later on November 3, 1919. The model was off by only four days in a forecast covering almost four years.

The movement from March 1938 to April 1940 must be treated as an upward phase. Its descending middle section was the break early in 1939 [Figure 1.15a]. Of the two main sell-offs, the first was from January 5 to 26. The second

Using this model in isolation makes it difficult to see why Lindsay considered January 5 as the start of the sell-off and not earlier in November (11/12/38). Remember: *"a count from some previous turning point must expire within a few days of it"* (The turning point).

An easier answer is found in understanding his most famous model, Three Peaks and a Domed House. The January date was a perfect 222-day count from the final low of the base in the 3PDh pattern.

was from March 10 to April 11. The rise from February 21 to March 10 was the last rally. The last rally but one began on January 27. Its top formed a line, which continued until February 18. Point E was February 16, 1939, the last peak day in the line.

Jul Aug Sep Oct Nov Dec 1939 Feb Mar Apr May Jun

Figure 1.15a   *1939* Descending Middle Section

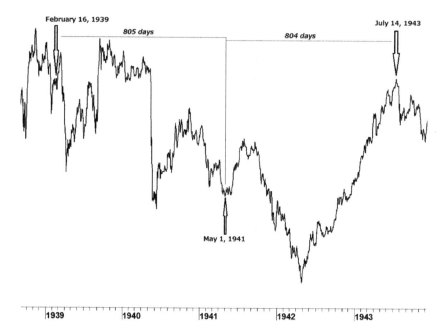

Figure 1.15b   *1939 Descending Middle Section*

In Figure 1.15b point E of the descending middle section on February 16, 1939 counts 805 days to the low of May 1, 1941. The high of the next advance was 805 days after that low. Why the market saw a lower low (than May 1, 1941) is addressed in chapter 2.

Point E also played a role in forecasting a low later that month on May 31, 1941 and can be found in Table 1.

ASCENDING MIDDLE SECTIONS

In ascending middle sections, the rally that touches the highest level is always considered the last rally, and point E falls in the last rally but two. In the middle section of March-July 1945 [Figure 1.16], the last rally was from May 24 to 29. The last rally but one was from May 10 to 19. The rise from March 26 to May 7 was the last rally but two. The pattern of a strong rally followed by two weaker ones is found elsewhere. The rail average formed one between September 1908 and February 1909. There was another in the industrials from October 1927 to February 1928. Point E was, in each case, the high day of the strong rally. It fell respectively, on November 17, 1908; November 30, 1927 [Figure 1.17]; and May 7, 1945.

> Point E is the top of the second-to-last rally and, in this example, falls on May 7, 1945.
>
> *Pattern of a strong rally followed by two weaker ones*: In a newsletter, decades later, Lindsay wrote the seemingly contradictory statement that when one rally (of the three) is smaller than the others, it is invariably the rally ending at point E.

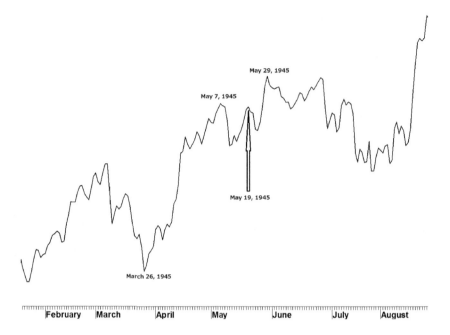

Figure 1.16   *1945 Ascending Middle Section*

Figure 1.17   *1927 Ascending Middle Section*

Another common pattern is illustrated by the ascending middle section of the 1934-1937 advance [Figure 1.18a]. The first reaction was from November to December 1935. The second reaction was in April 1936. There were sharp

> At first it seems Lindsay will identify March 6, 1936 as point E. But that was not to be. Continue reading.

rallies from February 26 to March 6, from March 13 to 26, and from March 28 to April 6. Another rally began on January 21.

After February 1, the angle of the ascent flattened. A labored climb continued for three weeks. Point E is always the high day of the flattened rally which precedes several steeper rallies. It is immaterial whether there are two or three sharp rallies. Point E was February 19, 1936, the high day of the struggling rally.

> *Point E is always the high day of the flattened rally which precedes several steeper rallies. It is immaterial whether there are two or three sharp rallies.* This comment is fascinating as Lindsay makes no mention of it in his "Counts from the Middle Section" newsletter published in 1983 by Investors Intelligence.

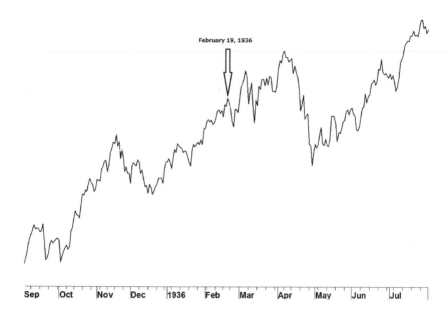

Figure 1.18a   *1935-1936 Ascending Middle Section*

Figure 1.18b   *1936 Ascending Middle Section*

In figure 1.18b point E, the high day of the ascending middle section's flattened top, counts 385 days to the top of the bull market on March 10, 1937. The bear market low, March 31, 1938, lies only one day later than the equidistance would imply.

Note that this point E (February 19, 1936) of an ascending middle section is only three days after point E of the descending middle section on February 16 shown in Figure 1.15b.

The industrial average was in an irregular uptrend from October 1946 to June 1948 [Figure 1.19a]. The first reaction of its ascending middle section was from February to May 1947. The second reaction was from July 1947 to February 1948. The rallies were not proportionate to the length of the whole formation, but they were the only rallies available. The last was from July 18 to 25. The last rally but one was from June 25 to July 14. The last rally but two ended on June 23, 1947. This day was point E.

In Figure 1.19b counting from point E on June 23, 1947 to the top of the bull market on June 1, 1948 is 357 days. The bear market bottom on June 13, 1949 was 364 days later.

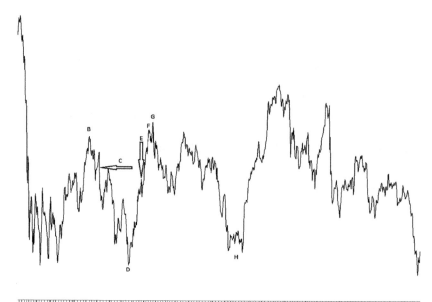

Figure 1.19a   *1947-1948 Ascending Middle Section*

Figure 1.19b   *1947-1948 Ascending Middle Section*

The rise of 1917-1919 had an ascending middle section [Figure 1.20a]. The first reaction was in August-September 1918. The second reaction was from October 1918 to January 1919. The last rally was from October 9 to 19. The last rally but one was from September 13 to October 4. When an ascending middle section has only two rallies in all, point E is the second daily peak in the minor fluctuations of the first rally. The rise of September 14 was followed by a one day dip. Another small gain ended on September 18. Point E was September 18, 1918.

Importantly, Lindsay views the time between points D and F in this example to be a single rally.

Point G was October 19, 1918 (full moon).

Point F was October 4, 1918 (new moon).

Point E was September 18, 1918.

The pullback from point G is typically longer than the pullback following point F.

Allowing for only two rallies in an ascending middle section was another addition to Lindsay's 1983 newsletter description of counts from middle sections.

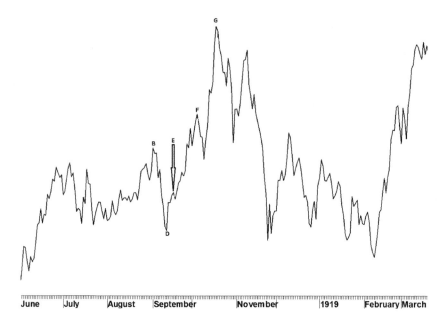

Figure 1.20a   *1918-1919 Ascending Middle Section*

Sometimes the division of the rallies is not clear. There may be many sell-offs of varying depth, so that it is difficult to tell when the rally containing point E begins and ends. Reference should be made to another middle section in past markets which had a similar price pattern. Point E will fall in an analogous position in both cases.

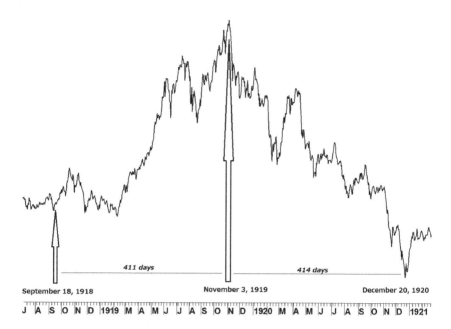

411 days

414 days

September 18, 1918   November 3, 1919   December 20, 1920

J A S O N D 1919 M A M J J A S O N D 1920 M A M J J A S O N D 1921

Figure 1.20b   *1918-1919 Ascending Middle Section*

In Figure 1.20b point E on September 18, 1919 counts 411 days to the bull market high on November 3, 1919. The following bear market low is 414 days after that high.

THE METHOD OF COUNTING

The number of calendar days is counted backward from the turning point to point E. If there is some definite reason which makes a count to point E impracticable, the measurement is continued until it reaches point C. The identical number of days is then counted forward from the same turning point. The result is a date in the future. If the turning point was a high, a low will fall on the future date, or within a few days of it. If the turning point was a low, a high will come on or near the projected date.

"*...some definite reason which makes a count to point E impracticable...*" typically means the count conflicts with another Lindsay model as we saw in Figure 1.15a or it fails to match a standard time span (chapter 5).

A 'turning point' is labeled as point A or point J in Lindsay's typical schemes.

We cannot use the middle section to compute the high of the bull market in which it occurs. It must be used to calculate the time of the next bear market low or the high of the next bull market after that low.

All counts from middle sections are equidistances in time. If the equidistance is centered on a low turning point, the result will be a high. If it is centered on a high, the result will be a low.

For example, if a count is started at the bull market high of March 10, 1937, it will be found that point E on February 19, 1936, was 385 days earlier [Figure 1.21]. When the same number of days is counted forward the projected date of an important low is March 30, 1938. The actual bear market low was one day later on March 31.

Figure 1.21   *1936 Ascending Middle Section*

Two measurements, one to a high and the other to a low, proceed from every uptrend. Often they are both counted to the same measuring point. On other occasions, the high may be equidistant from point C, for example, while the low is measured by point E. Every important high and low in history has been equidistant, or nearly so, from a point C or E. Many of the counts of the past are listed in the Tables. Those in Tables 1 and 2, on pages 6 and 7 [pages 52 and 53] are called the basic cycle to distinguish them from another series of measurements.

> Translation: Every middle section counts to a high at point J and a low at point A. These counts may be taken from both point E and point C, or from only one of the two points.

The great insight which Lindsay brought to the fore was that all advances and declines tend to cluster together into groups of similar duration. He called these groups the Standard Time Spans and used their durations to identify what he later called, basic movements (basic advances and basic declines).

The 'counts' which comprise the next to last columns in Tables 1 and 2 seem to fit, for the most part, into Lindsay's Standard Time Spans. The counts from point J to point A in Table 1 (Basic Equidistances Ending at a Low) fit into the Standard Time spans for basic declines. The counts from point A to point J in Table 2 (Basic Equidistances Ending at a High) fit into the Standard Time Spans for basic advances. A table of the Standard Time Spans can be found at the end of this chapter. See chapter 5 for a more detailed explanation.

A basic cycle is the time period between a measuring point and a turning point together with the time period following the turning point (a basic advance or decline). Lindsay writes that these counts have been adjusted to fit the major cycle. By "unadjusted" he means the counts do not necessarily account for such concepts as secondary lows and sideways movements. Therefore the second half of each basic cycle (an advance or decline) may, or may not, reflect the counts shown in the table of standard time spans later in this chapter.

TABLE 1   BASIC EQUIDISTANCES ENDING AT A LOW

TO POINT C	TO POINT E	NO. DAYS	FROM POINT J	NO. DAYS	TO POINT A	
	Jul 31, 1885	490	Dec 3, 1886	486	Apr 2, 1888	
	Nov 16, 1889	191	May 26, 1890	196	Dec 8, 1890	
	Oct 6, 1894	333	Sep 4, 1895	339	Aug 8, 1896	
	Jan 13, 1898	445	Apr 3, 1899	446	Jun 23, 1900	R
	Jul 29, 1901	407	Sep 9, 1902	403	Oct 15, 1903	
Jul 8, 1901		428	Sep 9, 1902	428	Nov 9, 1903	
	Mar 23, 1904	670	Jan 22, 1906	668	Nov 21, 1907	R
	Nov 17, 1908	307	Sep 20, 1909	309	Jul 26, 1910	R
	Dec 9, 1908	297	Oct 2, 1909	297	Jul 26, 1910	I
	Jan 20, 1912	254	Sep 30, 1912	254	Jun 11, 1913	
Oct 24, 1910		707	Sep 30, 1912	715	Sep 15, 1914	
Oct 27, 1915*		391	Nov 21, 1916	393	Dec 19, 1917	
	Sep 18, 1918	411	Nov 3, 1919	414	Dec 21, 1920	
Jan 11, 1918		661	Nov 3, 1919	661	Aug 25, 1921	
	Aug 7, 1922	225	Mar 20, 1923	221	Oct 27, 1923	
	Dec 24, 1925	49	Feb 11, 1926	47	Mar 30, 1926	
	Jan 3, 1923	1135	Feb 11, 1926	1139	Mar 26, 1929	
	Nov 30, 1927	643	Sep 3, 1929	637	Jun 2, 1931	
	Oct 28, 1926*	1041	Sep 3, 1929	1039	Jul 8, 1932	
	Aug 25, 1933	164	Feb 5, 1934	171	Jul 26, 1934	
	Feb 19, 1936	385	Mar 10, 1937	386	Mar 31, 1938	
	Feb 16, 1939	417	Apr 8, 1940	418	May 31, 1941	
	Feb 25, 1943	139	Jul 14, 1943	139	Nov 30, 1943	
	Dec 27, 1945	153	May 29, 1946	154	Oct 30, 1946	I
	Jul 10, 1945	342	Jun 17, 1946	336	May 19, 1947	R
	Jun 23, 1947	357	Jun 14, 1948	364	Jun 13, 1949	

*New York Times average   The letters R and I denote rails and industrials

6

Table 1   *Basic Equidistances Ending at Low*

TABLE 2   BASIC EQUIDISTANCES ENDING AT A HIGH

~~TO POINT C~~	TO POINT E	NO. DAYS	FROM POINT A	NO. DAYS	TO POINT J
	Feb 13, 1886	779	Apr 2, 1888	771	
	Jun 15, 1891	772	Jul 26, 1893	770	Sep 4, 1895
Dec 9, 1893		973	Aug 8, 1896	968	Apr 3, 1899 R
	Mar 30, 1898	815	Jun 23, 1900	808	Sep 9, 1902
Jul 8, 1901		829	Oct 15, 1903	827	Jan 19, 1906
	Nov 1, 1905	744	Nov 15, 1907	735	Nov 19, 1909 I
May 19, 1908		798	Jul 26, 1910	797	Sep 30, 1912 I
May 3, 1912		404	Jun 11, 1913	406	Jul 22, 1914 I
Nov 28, 1910		926	Jun 11, 1913	929	Dec 27, 1915 I
Dec 1, 1911		745	Dec 15, 1913	742	Dec 27, 1915 I
	Jan 9, 1911*	1071	Dec 15, 1913	1071	Nov 20, 1916
	Feb 10, 1916*	679	Dec 20, 1917	683	Nov 3, 1919
	Sep 18, 1918	825	Dec 21, 1920	819	Mar 20, 1923
	Jul 7, 1921*	842	Oct 27, 1923	840	Feb 13, 1926
Oct 23, 1922		1254	Mar 30, 1926	1253	Sep 3, 1929
	Oct 1, 1928*	176	Mar 26, 1929	177	Sep 19, 1929
	Apr 12, 1929	781	Jun 2, 1931	777	Jul 18, 1933
	Dec 2, 1930	584	Jul 8, 1932	577	Feb 5, 1934
	Jan 14, 1932	924	Jul 26, 1934	923	Feb 3, 1937
	Feb 19, 1936	771	Mar 31, 1938	770	May 9, 1940
	Feb 16, 1939	805	May 1, 1941	804	Jul 14, 1943
Sep 25, 1941		796	Nov 30, 1943	795	Feb 2, 1946
Mar 8, 1945		601	Oct 30, 1946	593	Jun 14, 1948
	Oct 20, 1947	602	Jun 13, 1949		?
	Jun 23, 1947	721	Jun 13, 1949		?
Mar 7, 1947		829	Jun 13, 1949		?

*New York Times industrials

7

Table 2   *Basic Equidistances Ending at a High*

MAJOR MIDDLE SECTIONS

There are trends that last a longer time than the advances of the basic cycle. They form correspondingly larger middle sections. Each individual rally must be a separate trend apparent on a weekly chart, but its duration is variable. No matter whether a middle section lasts ten days or ten years, the measuring points are located in exactly the same manner.

In the rise from 1896 to 1906, the industrials traced an ascending middle section [Figure 1.22]. The first reaction was the bear market of 1899-1900. The second

> The rise from 1896 to 1906 is the advance of the first multiple cycle in the sixth long cycle shown in Figure 2.1 in chapter 2.

reaction was the decline of 1901-1903. The last rally was from May 9 to June 17, 1901. The last rally but one was from February 28 to May 1. The last rally but two ended on February 15, 1901. This day became point E. The first reaction began at the bull market high of September 5, 1899. September 11, the first weak day thereafter, was point C. December 8, 1899, after the final top, was also a possible point C.

Figure 1.22   *1899-1901 Ascending Middle Section*

In the uptrend from 1921 to 1929, the first reaction of the ascending middle section was the bear market of 1923 [Figure 1.23]. The second reaction was the break of 1926. The last rally was from April 1925 to February 1926. The last rally but one was from October 1924 to March 1925. The last rally but two began in May and ended on August 20, 1924. This day became point E. Point C was April 30, 1923, the first day in the first reaction that was as weak as any day to follow.

Point E, in the next-to-last rally, fell on August 20, 1924.

Point C, the day of the break under the minor top formation (at the beginning of the first reaction) was on April 30, 1923. That date was also a full moon.

February 11, 1926 was the day before a new moon.

Figure 1.23   *1922-1926 Ascending Middle Section*

The rise from 1921 to 1926 may be taken as a unit. The first reaction of its ascending middle section was from October to November 1922 [Figure 1.24]. The second reaction was the bear market of 1923. Two principal rallies followed the low of January 17, 1923. The advance after November 29, 1922, started strongly. But after

> The rise from 1921 to 1926 is comprised of a complete basic cycle from 1921 to 1924 along with the advancing portion of the next basic cycle, 1924-1926.
>
> Point E was January 3, 1923.
>
> Point C was October 23, 1922.

December 8, the ascent was labored for nearly a month. Point E was the high day of the flattened rally, January 3, 1923. Point C was October 23, 1922, the first really weak day.

Figure 1.24   *1922-1923 Ascending Middle Section*

In the uptrend from 1923 to 1929, any two widely
spaced reactions define an ascending middle
section, provided no other sell-off as deep comes
between them.

An uptrend stretched from 1914 to 1929. The bear market of 1917 was the first reaction of its ascending middle section. The decline of 1919-1921 was the second. The rise of 1919 consisted of two sharp upthrusts. The rally of September-October 1918 was also brisk. But the rally that began in May 1918 dragged out at the same level for months. As always, point E was the high day of the flattened rally. It was August 26, 1918, according to the New York Times average.

The 1914-1929 advance comprises most of the long cycle of 1914-1932 as illustrated in Figure 2.1 in chapter 2.

Rational people can disagree on whether January 2, 1934 is the end of a rally or not. But any disagreement is seemingly academic given Lindsay's statement that *Point E is always the high day of the flattened rally which precedes several steeper rallies. It is immaterial whether there are two or three sharp rallies.*

Point E was December 9, 1933

Point C was July 19, 1933

In the advance from 1932 to 1937, the break of July-October 1933 [Figure 1.25] was the first reaction of the ascending middle section. The decline from February to July 1934 was the second. The last rally was from January 8 to February 5, 1934. The last rally but one was from December 20, 1933, to January 2, 1934. The last rally but two had the typical flattened top. The high day was December 9, 1933, which became point E. Point C was July 19, 1933, the first weak day in the first reaction.

The 1932-1937 advance was comprised of the first complete basic cycle, and the advancing portion of the second basic cycle, in the first multiple cycle of the final long cycle shown in Figure 2.1 in chapter 2.

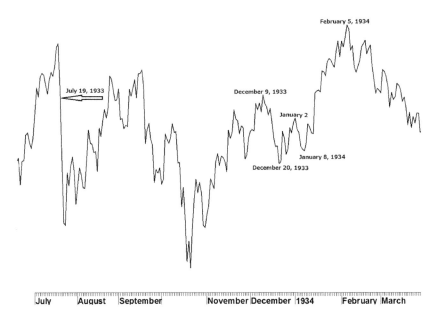

Figure 1.25   *1933-1934 Ascending Middle Section*

In the advance of 1942-1946, an ascending middle section started at the sharp break of April 6-13, 1943 [Figure 1.26]. The second reaction was the decline from July to November 1943. The last rally was from June 22 to July 14. The last rally but one was from May 14 to June 5. Point E was May 10, 1943, the high day of the last rally but two. Point C was April 9, 1943, the only really weak day in the first reaction.

July 14, 1943 was point G.

June 5, 1943 was point F.

May 10, 1943 was point E.

April 9, 1943 was point C.

The 1942-1946 advance was the first complete basic cycle, and the advancing portion of the next basic cycle, in the second multiple cycle, of the final long cycle shown in Figure 2.1 in chapter 2.

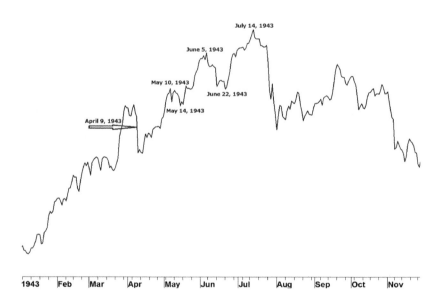

Figure 1.26   *1943 Ascending Middle Section*

A count to one of the above middle sections must, as a minimum, cover the time occupied by one complete basic cycle and part of another one. These counts comprise the major cycle, as distinguished from the basic cycle. Some of them are

Reminder: Here Lindsay is referring to major middle sections found in major cycles and not the smaller basic cycles found contained with basic movements discussed earlier in the chapter.

A complete basic cycle is composed of one basic advance and one basic decline. This is covered in chapter 2.

listed in Tables 3 and 4 [chapter 2]. The basic and major cycles operate on different scales, but according to exactly the same principles.

Standard Time Spans

	Advances	Declines
Subnormal	414-615	222-250
Short	630-718	317-364
Long	742-830	376-446
Extended	929-968	N/A

Review Notes

The counting method uses calendar days and is applicable to more than just equities.

A middle section is the time period between points B and H in the Typical Schemes. It is a period in a bull market in which the rate of ascent slows or even declines. It is "book-ended" by two distinct declines (reactions) in the averages.

Reactions: the declines surrounding a middle section

Turning Point: An important counting date *not* inside the middle section. A turning point is a price extreme – "the highest or lowest level" – meaning the intraday high or low. These dates are designated as points A and J in the Typical Schemes.

There are two measuring points in every middle section. In the Typical Schemes, they are represented by the letters C and E.

Point E is the next-to-last rally in a descending middle section and the second-to-last rally in an ascending middle section. In a descending middle section, if the time surrounding the next-to-last rally forms a consolidation or "line", point E is the final high in the consolidation.

Point C is the first day the average breaks down below the minor top formation surrounding point B. If the high before the first reaction was a multiple top, a point C may follow any or all of the peaks.

In a descending middle section there are two rallies of interest and they are labeled points E and G. In an ascending middle section there may be many rallies but only the final three are of interest and they are labeled points E, F, and G.

An Aid to Timing

Chapter 2

Ed Carlson

2. An Aid to Timing

THE HIGH OF THE MULTIPLE CYCLE

The chart on page 9 [Figure 2.1 on page 66] shows every basic cycle of the past. The declining portion of each one has been drawn as a dotted line. From two to four basic cycles comprise a multiple cycle. It is usually separated from other multiple cycles by a drastic or long drawn out bear market. On each of the eight rows of the chart, there are two multiple cycles. The lows of 1805, 1829, 1848, 1865, 1884, 1903, 1921, and 1942 mark the dividing line. The two multiple cycles on each row together form one long cycle.

Long Cycle

Multiple Cycle   Multiple Cycle

2-4 Basic Cycles   2-4 Basic Cycles

One basic cycle contains one basic advance + one basic decline. The "dotted line" Lindsay refers to contains a basic decline but is not always limited to the time span of a basic decline. The same applies to the advancing portion of a basic cycle and basic advances. For more info on basic advances and basic declines see chapter five.

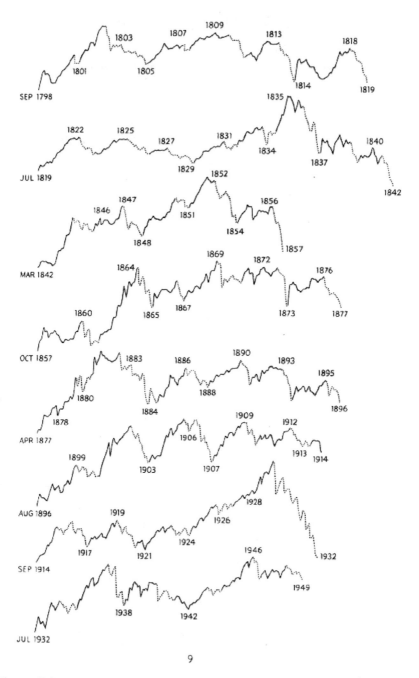

9

Figure 2.1   *Long Cycles*

The long cycles Lindsay showed in Figure 2.1 may be better understood by choosing one of the long cycles in Figure 2.1 and examining each basic advance and decline within each basic cycle. The long cycle of 1914-1932 provides a relatively simple example (Figure 2.2). A review of the basic movements can be found in chapter five.

Lindsay appears to have ignored the market's "swan song" in 1914 caused by WWI and the closing of the stock exchange from August 1, 1914 to December 12, 1914. He counts the basic advance to the December 27, 1915 high from the low of June 11, 1913. It counts as an extended basic advance of 929 days (chapter five, standard time spans). The time period between December 27, 1915 and the ultimate high on November 21, 1916 is a sideways movement . The November 21, 1916 high is a short 15year interval of 14years, 11months from the low of December 24, 1901. For a review of the long-term intervals and sideways movements refer to chapter five.

Counting from the November 21, 1916 market top to the low on December 19, 1917 is a long basic decline of 393 days and is a short 12year interval of 11years, 11months from the high of January 19, 1906.

The high of November 3, 1919 makes up for lost time in the previous long term intervals as, at 16 years, it is a long 15year interval from the November 9, 1903 low. As anticipated by the Principle of Alternation, it was a short basic advance from December 19, 1917 of 684 days. For more on the Principle of Alternation see chapter five.

The November 3, 1919 high counts a long basic decline of 414 days to the secondary low on December 21, 1920. This is an example of the basic cycle not matching the basic movements. For more information on secondary lows see chapter five.

Counting the next basic advance from the December 21, 1920 secondary low is a long basic advance of 819 days to the high on March 20, 1923. This high is 15years, 4months from the low of November 15, 1907.

The March 20, 1923 high counts a long basic decline of 427 days to another secondary low on May 20, 1924 which is 12years, 11months from the June 7, 1911 high. The lower and earlier low, on October 27, 1923, was 12years, 5months from the 1911 high and counts a perfect 221 days from the March 1923 top. Lindsay wrote that the time interval of 221-225 days appears throughout the history of the Dow Industrials.

From the May 20, 1924 bottom the market advanced 632 days (a short basic advance) to the February 11, 1926 top. This top, at only 14years, 4months from the September 25, 1911 low, was destined to be a sideways movement. Unlike the majority of sideways movements it was not destined to be a top in the market. In this case the market advanced out of the sideways movement which foretold the terrible bear market which was to come in 1929.

The sideways movement was a short basic decline of 348 days to the low on January 25, 1927. From there the market advanced for 952 days (an extended basic advance) to the September 3, 1929 high. This high was a short 15 year interval from the December 4, 1914 low of 14years, 8months.

Lindsay labeled the time between the 1929 and 1930 highs as another sideways movement; an almost-perfect interval of 226 days. The 1930 high is 15years, 4months from the December 1914 low. The period between the high on April 17, 1930 and the June 2, 1931 low was 411 days – a long basic decline. The decline following the bounce in June 1930 was a long basic decline of 376 days from June 27, 1931 to July 8, 1932. The 1932 low was 12years, 8months from the November 3, 1919 high.

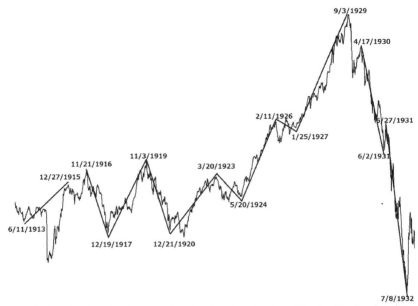

Figure 2.2   *1914-1932 Long Cycle*

The highest price in the second multiple cycle in each row may fall in any one of its three or four component basic cycles. To compute the date, an equidistance is taken from the longest ascending middle section available. If there was no ascending middle section of major proportions, the longest descending middle section is used. The uptrend of which the middle section

> Here Lindsay explains how to count to a very specific point in the long cycle; the highest price in the second multiple cycle.
>
> A middle section of "*major proportions*" is a middle section which encompasses more than just one basic advance or decline.

is a part may run through one, or portions of two, multiple cycles. Point A must be the last low day of the multiple cycle in which the uptrend ended.

When an equidistance is centered on point A in 1896, the longest ascending middle section

In this case, a forecast covering a period of over 20 years was off by a mere two days!

available was the one that extended from November 1885 to April 1888. Point E on July 3, 1886, was 3689 days before the low of August 8, 1896. The high in the railroad average on September 17, 1906, was 3691 days later. The price at this point was never afterward equaled in the same multiple cycle.

The multiple cycle is a cluster of several basic cycles. It does not have recognizable measuring points of its own. The major cycle is an independent movement, governed by middle sections, which is superimposed on the other two cycles. It may or may not coincide with them. The

This is as close to a definition of the major cycle as we get from Lindsay.

high of the multiple cycle is determined by the major cycle. Hence, the time it occurs bears no relation to the structure of the multiple cycle as a whole. In 1906, the high fell in the first basic cycle of the series. In 1809, 1852, 1869, 1890 and 1946, it came in the second. In 1835 and 1929, it was in the third. The counts ending at these highs are listed in Table 4 on page 11 [page 72]. In every case, they stem from the most decisive middle section available.

TABLE 3   MAJOR EQUIDISTANCES ENDING AT A LOW

TO POINT C	TO POINT E		FROM POINT J		TO POINT A
	November 1804	61 mo	December 1809	60 mo	December 1814
	June 1807	132 mo	June 1818	132 mo	June 1829
October 1802		188 mo	June 1818	188 mo	February 1834
	June 1828	83 mo	May 1835	82 mo	March 1842
	November 1832	96 mo	November 1840	96 mo	November 1848
	February 1848	58 mo	December 1852	58 mo	October 1857
	March 1846	81 mo	December 1852	80 mo	August 1859
February 1853		49 mo	March 1857	49 mo	Apr 20, 1861
June 1844		152 mo	February 1857	152 mo	Sep 29, 1869
	Dec 14, 1864	1631 da	Jun 2, 1869	1619 da	Nov 7, 1873
	Feb 27, 1867	3260 da	Jan 31, 1876	3255 da	Dec 29, 1884
	May 18, 1864	4275 da	Jan 31, 1876	4275 da	Oct 15, 1887
	Feb 27, 1861	5451 da	Jan 31, 1876	5425 da	Dec 8, 1890
	Apr 9, 1887	1154 da	Jun 4, 1890	1148 da	Jul 26, 1893
	Feb 21, 1884	2277 da	May 17, 1890	2275 da	Aug 8, 1896
	Jun 15, 1883	2528 da	May 17, 1890	2529 da	Apr 19, 1897
	Aug 16, 1890	1845 da	Sep 4, 1895	1846 da	Sep 24, 1900
	Aug 16, 1887	2941 da	Sep 4, 1895	2945 da	Sep 28, 1903 R
	Jun 15, 1883	4464 da	Sep 4, 1895	4460 da	Nov 21, 1907 R
	Nov 3, 1880	5418 da	Sep 4, 1895	5438 da	Jul 26, 1910
	Aug 26, 1898	2702 da	Jan 19, 1906	2700 da	Jun 11, 1913 I
	Aug 26, 1898	2943 da	Sep 17, 1906	2920 da	Sep 15, 1914 R
	Apr 22, 1896	3799 da	Sep 17, 1906	3799 da	Feb 10, 1917 R
	Jul 8, 1907	1911 da	Sep 30, 1912	1906 da	Dec 19, 1917 T
	Aug 31, 1903	3316 da	Sep 30, 1912	3304 da	Oct 17, 1921 I
	Feb 15, 1901	4245 da	Sep 30, 1912	4250 da	May 20, 1924 I
	Aug 26, 1898	5148 da	Sep 30, 1912	5133 da	Oct 20, 1926 :
Feb 25, 1907		4634 da	Nov 3, 1919	4631 da	Jul 8, 1932 I
Mar 1, 1926		1282 da	Sep 3, 1929	1273 da	Feb 27, 1933
	Aug 20, 1924	1840 da	Sep 3, 1929	1840 da	Sep 17, 1934
	Feb 16, 1921	3121 da	Sep 3, 1929	3131 da	Mar 31, 1938
Dec 12, 1916		4648 da	Sep 3, 1929	4620 da	Apr 28, 1942
	Jan 14, 1932	1882 da	Mar 10, 1937	1875 da	Apr 28, 1942
	Dec 9, 1933	1187 da	Mar 10, 1937	1188 da	Jun 10, 1940
Jul 19, 1933		1942 da	Nov 12, 1938	1941 da	Mar 6, 1944*
	Nov 25, 1930	2909 da	Nov 12, 1938	2909 da	Oct 30, 1946
	May 10, 1943	1115 da	May 29, 1946	1111 da	Jun 13, 1949
	Jan 10, 1941	1965 da	May 29, 1946		?
	Aug 20, 1924	5197 da	Nov 12, 1938		?
	Jan 10, 1941	2712 da	Jun 14, 1948		?
	Jan 15, 1938	3803 da	Jun 14, 1948		?

*Breakaway date. The actual secondary lows of February 7 and April 25, 1944, were the result of minor measurements.

10

Table 3   *Major Equidistances Ending at a Low*

TABLE 4 MAJOR EQUIDISTANCES ENDING AT A HIGH

TO POINT C	TO POINT E		FROM POINT A		TO POINT J
	April 1801	52 mo	August 1805	52 mo	December 1809
	September 1807	87 mo	December 1814	87 mo	March 1822
	September 1803	190 mo	July 1819	190 mo	May 1835
	June 1827	120 mo	June 1837	122 mo	August 1847
July 1831		128 mo	March 1842	129 mo	December 1852
	October 1844	49 mo	November 1848	49 mo	December 1852
	June 1827	177 mo	March 1842	177 mo	December 1856
	October 1840	97 mo	November 1848	97 mo	December 1856
	April 1851	78 mo	October 1857	78 mo	Apr 13, 1864
	March 1846	139 mo	October 1857	139 mo	Jun 2, 1869
	Jan 29, 1861	1520 da	Mar 29, 1865	1526 da	Jun 2, 1869
	Apr 28, 1866	1250 da	Sep 29, 1869	1244 da	Feb 24, 1873
	Apr 28, 1866	2750 da	Nov 7, 1873	2757 da	May 26, 1881
	Feb 27, 1867	3697 da	Apr 12, 1877	3688 da	May 18, 1887
Apr 16, 1864		4744 da	Apr 12, 1877	4783 da	May 17, 1890
	Aug 12, 1879	1966 da	Dec 29, 1884	1965 da	May 17, 1890
Jul 25, 1878		2160 da	Jun 23, 1884	2161 da	May 24, 1890
	Jun 15, 1883	1753 da	Apr 2, 1888	1755 da	Jan 21, 1893
Nov 21, 1885		2804 da	Jul 26, 1893	2835 da	May 1, 1901
	Jul 3, 1886	3689 da	Aug 8, 1896	3691 da	Sep 17, 1906 R
	Jun 15, 1883	4803 da	Aug 8, 1896	4802 da	Oct 2, 1909
Sep 21, 1897		2214 da	Oct 15, 1903	2212 da	Nov 4, 1909 I
	Jan 8, 1903	1772 da	Nov 15, 1907	1781 da	Sep 30, 1912
	Feb 15, 1901	2464 da	Nov 15, 1907	2441 da	Jul 22, 1914 I
Jan 18, 1907		2336 da	Jun 11, 1913	2336 da	Nov 3, 1919 I
	Mar 20, 1917	1619 da	Aug 25, 1921	1631 da	Feb 11, 1926
Sep 11, 1899		5482 da	Sep 15, 1914	5483 da	Sep 19, 1929
	Nov 7, 1927	1705 da	Jul 8, 1932	1706 da	Mar 10, 1937
	Oct 1, 1928	1376 da	Jul 8, 1932	1368 da	Apr 6, 1936
	Jun 2, 1927	1863 da	Jul 8, 1932	1863 da	Aug 14, 1937
Mar 1, 1926		2321 da	Jul 8, 1932	2318 da	Nov 12, 1938
	Aug 20, 1924	2879 da	Jul 8, 1932	2862 da	May 9, 1940
Apr 30, 1923		3357 da	Jul 8, 1932	3359 da	Sep 18, 1941
	Dec 9, 1933	1573 da	Mar 31, 1938	1574 da	Jul 22, 1942
	Aug 26, 1918	5065 da	Jul 8, 1932	5073 da	May 29, 1946
	Jan 15, 1938	1564 da	Apr 28, 1942	1568 da	Aug 13, 1946
	Feb 19, 1936	2260 da	Apr 28, 1942	2267 da	Jul 12, 1948
	Dec 9, 1933	3062 da	Apr 28, 1942		?
Jul 19, 1933		3205 da	Apr 28, 1942		?
	May 10, 1943	1269 da	Oct 30, 1946		?
	May 10, 1943	2226 da	Jun 13, 1949		?

The letters R and I denote rails and industrials respectively.

11

Table 4   *Major Equidistances Ending at a High*

MEASURING POINTS IN DOWNTRENDS

Highs and secondary lows are counted to long, ascending middle sections. Primary lows are equidistant from the shorter, descending middle sections. To compute a low, an ascending middle section, like that of 1916-1921, must be discarded. Each of the two bear markets – those of 1917 and 1920 – becomes by itself a separate descending middle section. The point marked L in the Typical Schemes serves as point E. In all bear markets, there are two or three successive rallies in the same general price range. They are separated from one another by only moderate declines. The entire sequence of rallies comes between two of the main waves of liquidation.

> Remember: Measuring points are the points E and C in a middle section. Turning points are points A and J.
>
> When Lindsay writes here that "Highs and secondary lows are counted to long, ascending middle sections" he is not referring to "turning points", but the later forecasted date in the future (end of the second equidistance).
>
> Looking at Tables 3 and 4, highs are forecast using ascending middle sections and lows are found using descending middle sections. However, exceptions do occur. For example, the high of November 1913 was found using point C (January 18, 1907) of a descending middle section.

Examples have been:

Mar 25, 1907 to Sep 21, 1907

Feb 2, 1917 to Jun 9, 1917

Dec 21, 1920 to May 7, 1921

Dec 17, 1931 to Mar 8, 1932

Nov 24, 1937 to Feb 23, 1938

Jun 10, 1940 to Sep 18, 1941

Nov 30, 1948 to May 4, 1949

Only the principal rallies are counted, and point E is in the last rally but one. In the industrial average, July 8, 1907; March 20, 1917; January 14, 1932; and January 15, 1938, were examples [Figures 2.3 - 2.7].

In these examples Lindsay is highlighting the time period between points K and M of the typical schemes.

In all bear markets, there are two or three successive rallies in the same general price range. They are separated from one another by only moderate declines. The entire sequence of rallies comes between two of the main waves of liquidation.

Figure 2.3   *Mar 25, 1907 to Sep 21 1907*

Figure 2.4   *Feb 2, 1917 to Jun 9, 1917*

Figure 2.5   *Dec 21, 1920 to May 7, 1921*

Figure 2.6   *Dec 17, 1931 to Mar 8, 1932*

January 15, 1938

Aug Sep Oct Nov Dec 1938 Feb Mar Apr May Jun Jul

Figure 2.7   *Nov 24, 1937 to Feb 23, 1938*

When the top of the rally forms a line, the last peak day in the line is tentatively considered point E. Examples were: February 16, 1921; January 10, 1941; and February 2, 1949. [Figures 2.5, 2.8, and 2.9] But any other peak day in the same line could also be point E.

"But any other peak day in the same line could also be point E." This comment explains Lindsay's choice of point E in Figure 2.3.

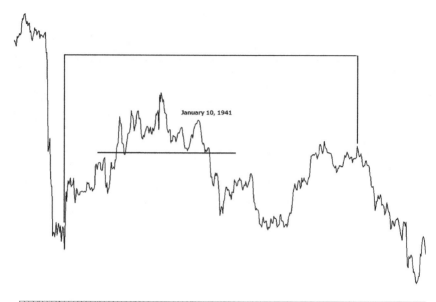

Figure 2.8   *June 10, 1940 to September 18, 1941*

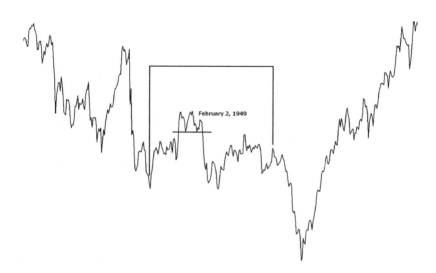

Figure 2.9   *Nov 30, 1948 to May 4, 1949*

If there is more than one sequence of rallies in the same bear market, each series is considered as a unit, and a point E may be found in any or all of them. Between November 10, 1930, and February 24, 1931, there were two rallies in the same price range. November 25 and December 2 were high days in the last rally but one. Either of them could have been point E [Figure 2.10].

Figure 2.10   *Nov 1930 – Feb 1931*

Take a look at Figure 2.1 to see where the interior bear market lows of 1917 and 1920 fall in the course of a long cycle.

When the final low of the long cycle is to be found, point J is the high of the second and final <u>multiple</u> cycle in the same long cycle.

When forecasting the low of an interior bear market (the low of a basic cycle within the long cycle), point J is found at the high of the previous long cycle's final <u>basic</u> cycle.

Here again Lindsay is explaining how to forecast very specific points in the long cycle.

Occasionally, the penultimate rally must be selected from all the rallies in the decline, regardless of whether they are in the same price range or not. Point E on August 31, 1903, was an example. This position is always the result of a conflict between two ways of counting. Point C is the first drastically weak day in the main wave of liquidation which precedes the series of rallies. December 12, 1916, was an example. In the industrial average, either January 18 or February 25, 1907 could have been point C. Measuring points in a bear market may time both the highs and lows of the future but more often the lows. They may operate in either the basic or the major cycle, usually the latter.

LINKED EQUIDISTANCES

A decline like that of 1890-1896, which closes a long cycle, is a terminal bear market. The declines that occur during the course of a long cycle, such as those of 1917 and 1920, are interior bear markets. When the low of a terminal bear market is to be counted, point J is the high of the same multiple cycle. When the low of an interior bear market is to be found, point J is the high day of the last basic cycle in the previous long cycle. These highs have fallen in 1818, 1840, 1856, 1876, 1895, 1912 and 1929. It will be explained later why the highs of 1938 and 1948 may both belong in the group.

From this high, the count goes back to point E (rarely C) in an interior bear market. The same number of days, when counted forward, arrives at or near the low of an interior bear market in the next long cycle. For instance, point E on February 16, 1921, was 3,121 days before the high of September 3, 1929. The bear market low of March 31, 1938, was 3,131 days afterward [Figure 2.11].

> The 1938 low was part of a long cycle that began at the 1932 low (see Figure 2.1). In this case, the high of the last basic cycle in the previous long cycle, or point J, was the high in 1929.
>
> The count missed the correct bottom by 10 days in a forecast which covered a period of 17 years.

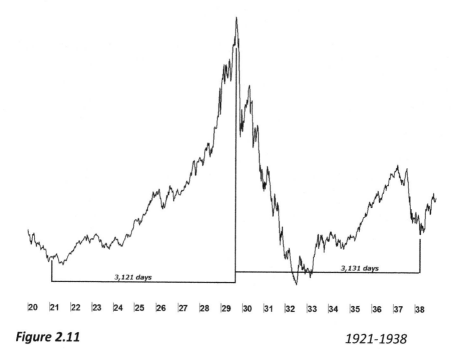

Figure 2.11   *1921-1938*

In like manner, the low of every other interior
bear market has been timed by a point E in some
previous decline of the same type. The successive
counts interlock one another and may be said to
form chains. One chain linked the declines ending
in 1848, 1865, 1888, 1903, 1921 and 1938. Another
series connected bear markets ending in 1829,
1854, 1861, 1890 and 1900. A third sequence began
in 1867 and may be traced through 1884, 1907,
1917 and 1942. Many of the counts are listed in
Table 3.

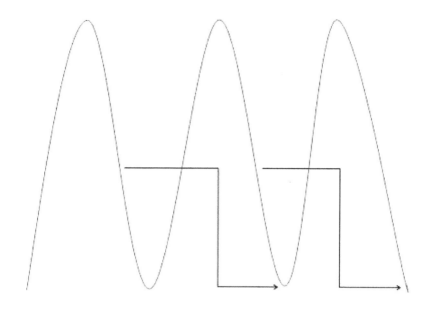

Figure 2.12   *Generic Chains*

It is best to begin with an understanding of the basic cycles and their basic movements in the second multiple cycle of the 1896-1914 long cycle (Figure 2.1). 1903–1914 was the second multiple cycle in the long cycle that extends from 1896-1914 (Figure 2.1).

The first basic cycle (of the second multiple cycle) can be divided into a basic advance which began on November 19, 1903 and lasted 802 days (a long basic advance) until the high on January 19, 1906.

The 1906 high was followed by two basic declines; a long basic decline of 430 days to the August 25, 1907 low and another long basic decline of 402 days from the October 9, 1906 high to the November 15, 1907 low at the bottom of the basic cycle.

The second basic cycle of this multiple cycle starts with a long basic advance of 687 days from the November 15, 1907 low to the October 2, 1909 high.

A count from the high in October, 1909 to the July 26, 1910 low was a subnormal basic decline of 297 days and concluded the second basic cycle of the second multiple cycle. Lindsay also counted a short basic decline of 342 days extending from the October 18, 1910 high to the low on September 25, 1911 which matches up with a 12year interval from September 5, 1899 (not shown).

The third basic cycle began with a long basic advance of 796 days from the 1910 low to the high of September 30, 1912.

That basic advance was, in turn, followed by a subnormal basic decline of 254 days to the June 11, 1913 low or a long basic decline of 443 days to the secondary low on December 15, 1913. As mentioned previously, Lindsay chose to ignore the time in late 1914 when the exchange was closed by World War I when counting the basic movements.

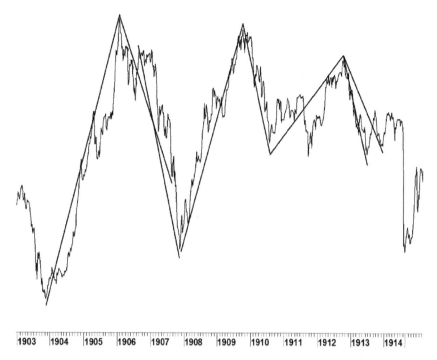

Figure 2.13   *Basic Movements 1903-1913*

Looking for the high of the last basic cycle of the previous long cycle (pre-1914) in Figure 2.13 it is found at the high of September 30, 1912 (point J is the high of the last basic cycle of the previous long cycle). This was the end of a long basic advance lasting 796 days originating on July 26, 1910 and becomes point J. It is from this point that we count backwards to a middle section to determine a count forward in time to an interior low (Figure 2.14).

Point E on July 8, 1907 counts 1,911 days to point J on September 30, 1912. Counting forward another 1,911 days is five days past the low of the first basic cycle, December 19, 1917, of the 1914-1932 long cycle.

Counting from the September high in 1912 to the middle section in 1903, point E on August 31 counts 3,318 days. Counting forward from the 1912 high the same number of days overshoots the August low in 1921. Lindsay shows a count of 3,304 days to a minor low on October 17, 1921. Of great interest, however, is that a count from the very significant low of November 19, 1903 counts 3,238 days to the high in 1912. Counting forward another 3,238 is only twelve days shy of the August 24, 1921 low. Lindsay would have referred to this phenomenon as a 'mirror image'.

In counting to a point E on February 15, 1901 Lindsay is using a short ascending middle section to count to a secondary low on May 20, 1924. The count between point E and the high in 1912 is 4,245 days. The May 20, 1924 secondary low came five days late at 4,250 days.

Point E (of an ascending middle section) on August 26, 1898 counts 5,148 days to the 1912 high. The secondary low of October 20, 1926 is found 5,133 days after the 1912 high.

All the counts begin from measuring points in the previous long cycle (1896-1914) and forecast an internal low in the next long cycle (1914-1932). All the internal lows forecast in the second long cycle use the turning point of September 30, 1912 which is the high of the last basic cycle in the previous long cycle (pre-1914).

The chart below is a weekly chart. When examining the middle sections in detail it is best to use a daily chart.

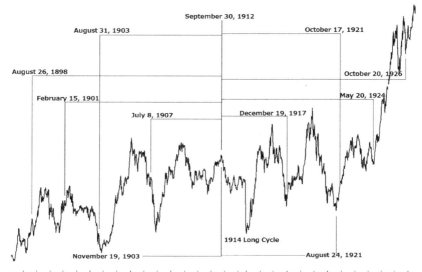

Figure 2.14   *September 30, 1912*

The 1942 low is the beginning of the second multiple cycle in the long cycle stretching from 1932 to 1949 (final example in Figure 2.1). Using Lindsay's guidelines, an internal low in this long cycle should be counted using the high of the final basic cycle in the previous long cycle, 13 years prior, in September 1929. Lindsay did not show any examples using the high in 1929 to count to an internal low post-1942. He writes *"None of the chains of bear markets crossed the period from 1921 to 1929"* and explains that comment later in this chapter.

However, counting to the high of the final basic cycle in the previous <u>multiple</u> cycle yields some interesting results. The final basic cycle of the 1932-1942 multiple cycle stretches between the lows of 1938 and 1942 (see Figure 2.1). The high of the cycle is actually one long consolidation lasting from late 1938 to early 1940. Although Lindsay counts the basic advance from the 1938 low to the final high of the consolidation in April 1940, the ultimate high of the cycle fell on November 12, 1938.

The November high counts back 1,608 days to point E in a descending middle section on June 18, 1934. The low of April 9, 1943 is 1,609 days after the November high.

November 12, 1938 counts back 2,132 days to point E of a descending middle section on January 10, 1933. The low on September 14, 1944 is 2,133 days after the 1938 top.

Point E in a descending middle section on November 25, 1930 counts 2,909 days to the November 1938 high. The low of October 30, 1946 is exactly 2,909 days after the 1938 high.

Two severe bear markets have appeared regularly during the course of each long cycle. One of them has usually been in the first mentioned chain. Until 1890, the second series carried another. Since 1884, the decline in the third chain has been drastic. The chains, however, are not perpetual. They begin and end when an interior decline must be counted to an ascending middle section. This occurred in 1924, and the continuity from 1900 was broken.

The course of prices from 1896 to 1914 had nothing in common with the pattern between 1914 and 1932. The chart [Figure 2.1] shows the two long cycles to be dissimilar in timing, price movement, and duration of trend. One of the chief differences lies in the relation of the two severe bear markets to the high of the multiple cycle. The high of 1906 was unusually close to the lows of 1903 and 1907. The high of 1929 was far removed from the corresponding lows of 1917 and 1921. All six points were determined according to principles that have been set forth. None of the chains of bear markets crossed the period from 1921 to 1929. This long free interval before the scheduled high made the great bull market possible.

THE SHIFT

A trend usually has one middle section so clearly defined that it stands out on a chart. In the same trend there may also be one or more secondary middle sections. They are shorter and of less amplitude, but they have the identical structure of all middle sections.

If there is no reason to the contrary, the count goes to point E in the principal middle section. But sometimes the count in the basic cycle disagrees with the major equidistance. The two measurements may expire months apart. In such cases, the basic count is shifted. It goes either to point C in the same middle section or to point E or C in one of the secondary middle sections. That measuring point is correct which eliminates or reduces the discrepancy between the two cycles.

The goal is to find a forecast date on which both the major and minor middle sections agree.

If using point E in each middle section doesn't work, the first option is to shift to point C in the basic middle section.

The second alternative is to shift to point C of the major middle section.

This approach usually works but not always. An example is shown in the section on Cross Currents below.

Should the discrepancy still remain unclosed, a similar shift is made in the major count. The two cycles come as close to an agreement as their respective measuring points permit.

However, the discrepancy cannot be closed if the trends of the two cycles lack the required measuring points. In that case, and under one or two other conditions, the two cycles operate independently, each according to point E in its principal middle section.

AN EXAMPLE OF THE SHIFT

In the 1903-1906 advance, the principal middle section was clearly defined [Figure 2.15]. The first reaction was in December 1904. The second reaction was from April to May 1905. A weekly chart shows how the momentum of the rise was arrested during that period. This is the essence of a middle section. Point E on January 20, 1905, was a year before the high of the basic cycle in January 1906. The next low would ordinarily have been a year later in January 1907.

Note how during the time period of an ascending middle section the rate of ascent of the market slows relative to the slope both before and after the middle section. This is a very simple, yet important, requirement of middle sections which is often forgotten amongst all the details.

"The next low would ordinarily been a year later in January 1907". Lindsay's rule-of-thumb is to expect an advance of roughly two years followed by a decline of roughly one year. A high in January 1906 would have led one to expect a low in January 1907. In this case, however, a right shoulder developed in late 1906 which delayed the expected low by ten months.

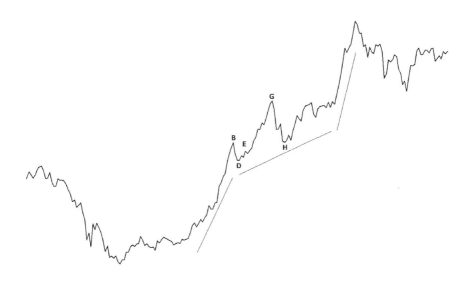

1903 | A | M | J | J | A | S | O | N | D | 1904 | A | M | J | J | A | S | O | N | D | 1905 | A | M | J | J | A | S | O | N | D | 1906 | A | M | J | J | A | S | O | N

Figure 2.15   _1905 Middle Section_

But the major equidistance from point E on July 3, 1886 (paragraph 2, page 8) [not shown], implied that the rails would not start to decline until September 1906. The major equidistance from point E on June 15, 1883 [not shown], indicated that they would continue to go down until November 1907. There was a

Here Lindsay, without explanation, changes the focus of analysis to the Dow Jones Transportation average. This index was often referred to as the "rails" during the early and mid-twentieth century due to the heavy weighting of railroads in the index at that time.

Point E on July 3, 1886 counted 10 years to point A in 1896. 10 years later would be expected to produce a high.

discrepancy between the two ways of counting.

The middle section from December 1904 to May 1905 must be discarded. The count is carried back to the next previous middle section in the same uptrend. There was only one other possible middle section in the earlier portion of the 1903-1906 rise.

In the rail average, the first reaction was from January 23 to March 14, 1904. The second reaction was from April 11 to May 16. Since the high of April did not equal that of January, the middle section was descending. The last rally was from March 25 to April 11. The last rally but one was from March 14 to 23. Point E was March 23, 1904, the high day of the penultimate rally. It was 670 days before the bull market high in rails, January 22, 1906. The bear market low was 668 days later on November 21, 1907.

The same low was 4,460 days after the last high of the previous multiple cycle, September 4, 1895. That date in turn, was 4,464 days after point E on June 15, 1883. The two ways of counting were in agreement.

Examining the Dow Industrials (rather than the Rails) the second to last high of a minor middle section (point E) was on 3/23/04 (Figure 2.16). It counted 670 days to the 1/19/06 bull market high. Counting forward another 670 days brings us to 11/20/07. The ultimate low of the 1906-07 bear market occurred on 11/15/07 at 53 and was followed by a test of that bottom on 11/22/07 at 53.08.

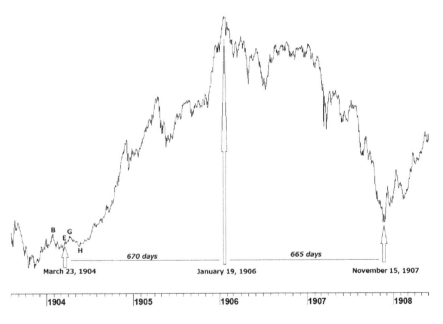

Figure 2.16   *1904 Middle Section*

CROSS CURRENTS

In some cases it is impossible to shift to another middle section so that the basic cycle will agree with the major count. Point C on March 1, 1926, was 2,321 days before the low of July 8, 1932 [Figure 2.17]. The high of November 12, 1938, was 2,318 days later. This major count turned the main trend down. But the basic cycle continued upward. No possible middle section in the 1934-1937 advance could give a count that would expire in 1938. The basic and major cycles must each work out according to its own measuring points. Until they agreed, the market would not move far or long in either direction.

In these examples Lindsay illustrates what can happen when the major and basic middle sections fail to agree in their forecasts.

Lindsay used the low of the long cycle (1932) as the turning point in this example. It counts to the high of the third basic cycle (1938-1942).

The descending middle section in 1926 is found just prior to the final basic cycle (1926-1932) in the previous long cycle (1914-1932).

From the basic low of March 31, 1938 a long basic advance of 739 days was counted to a high on April 8, 1940 (Figure 2.17). This basic advance is the advancing portion of the basic cycle Lindsay is referring to here ("*But the basic cycle continued upward.*").

This April 1940 high was lower than the high on November 12, 1938 forecast by the major middle section. While the time between the two separate highs was volatile, the 1938-1940 time span could be thought of as a major top formation particularly when compared to the drop which was to follow.

Figure 2.17   *1926-1938*

For the next five years there were no shifts. The
two cycles either agreed, or disagreed so evenly
that there was no advantage in a compromise.
Throughout the period, every turn in both cycles
was counted to the principal middle section, and
always to point E except in one case.

An equidistance
was now centered
on the low of
March 31, 1938.
Point E on
February 19,
1936, was 771

> Lindsay centered his turning point at
> the bottom of the 1938 basic cycle. The
> entire example is contained within one
> multiple cycle but the counts overlap
> two basic cycles.

days earlier. Exactly 771 days later, on May 10,
1940, the basic cycle turned down [Figure 2.18].
At this juncture, there was a major count that
tallied with it [see next example].

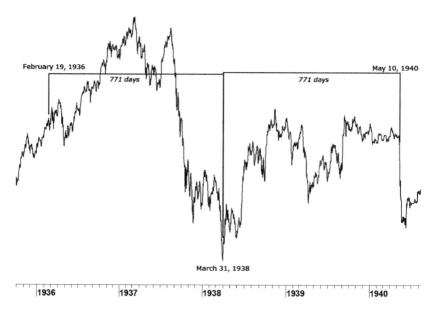

February 19, 1936   771 days   771 days   May 10, 1940

March 31, 1938

1936   1937   1938   1939   1940

Figure 2.18   *1936-1940*

The middle section of 1923-1926 was described on page 4 [Chapter 1, Major Middle Sections]. Point E on August 20, 1924, was 2879 days before the low of July 8, 1932. The break of May 10, 1940 was 2,863 days afterward [Figure 2.19].

In this example Lindsay again centers his equidistances on the 1932 low – the beginning of a new long cycle. His counts link five different basic cycles.

Note that the middle sections Lindsay presented here all point to the same top formation in 1940. The first middle section (Figure 2.17) counts to the day of the high whereas the second and third examples (Figures 2.18 and 2.19) count to the first impulsive day of decline.

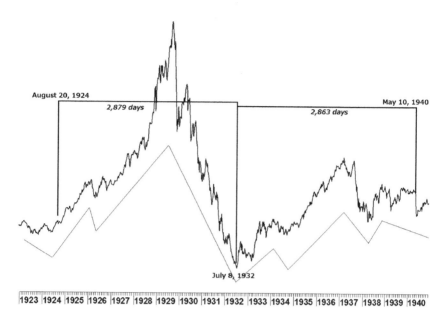

Figure 2.19   *1924-1940*

Lindsay's Principle of Continuity states that a new basic decline begins where the previous basic advance ended. The basic decline which began at the April 1940 high counted 388 days to a basic low on May 1, 1941 (not the June 1940 low shown in Figure 2.19). Note that the May 1941 low was not the end of the bear market nor was it lower than the June 1940 low identified by the middle section. The basic cycle did not end until a lower low was printed on April 28, 1942.

Here we see the counts centered on the high of the second basic cycle of the 1932-1942 multiple cycle. The entire count is contained within the multiple cycle.

The major middle section from July 1933 to July
1934 soon countered with a bullish equidistance
[Figure 2.20]. Point E on December 9, 1933, was
1,187 days before the high of March 10, 1937. The
low of June 10, 1940, was 1,188 days later.
Prices advanced, but not strongly, since the
basic cycle remained down. This caused renewed
selling after November 1940. But the June low was
not broken until a year and a half later, when
other major counts required it.

Figure 2.20   *1933-1940*

To determine when the basic cycle would turn up,
an equidistance was centered on the last clearly
defined high, April 8, 1940. It was 417 days
after point E on February 16, 1939. The last low
day of May 31, 1941, was 418 days afterward
[Figure 2.21].

Lindsay's choice of April 8, 1940 as a turning point may seem strange at first glance. A review of Figure 2.17 should provide the reader with a reminder of the significance of that date.

The entire count is contained within the 1938-1942 basic cycle.

Figure 2.21   *1939-1941*

The next advance had to be counted with May 1, 1941, as point A, since it was the low day of the line. Point E on February 16, 1939, was 805 days earlier. A rise must therefore continue for 805 days until July 15, 1943. Prices actually turned down on that day. During part of the time allotted to this advance in the basic cycle, however, the market met selling from the major cycle [Figure 2.22].

May 1, 1941 was the low of a long basic decline of 388 days from the April 8, 1940 high.

Lindsay is using the same middle section in this example he used in the previous example (Figure 2.21).

Lindsay explains the 1941-1942 decline by writing that *"the market met selling from the major cycle"*. The low in 1942 was the low between the multiple cycles in the 1932-1949 long cycle.

What he later came to call a 12-year interval pulled prices down into this time period. A 12-year interval is typically 12years, 2months to 12years, 8months and is counted from an important high (Chapter five, long-term intervals). The low on April 28, 1942 occurred 12years and 8months after the high of September 3, 1929. The low was timed by a descending middle section in 1932 (Figure 2.24).

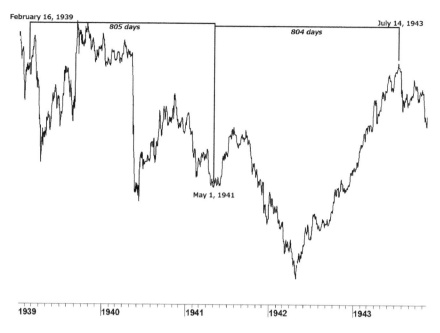

Figure 2.22   *1939-1943*

The break of May 1940 was timed by point E in August 1924 [Figure 2.19]. Point C in the same middle section was April 30, 1923. It was 3,357 days before the low of July 8, 1932. The last high of September 18, 1941, was 3,359 days later. This was one of many

Point E on August 20, 1924 counts 2,879 days to the low on July 8, 1932. The *"break of May 1940"* (Figure 2.19) began on May 9, seventeen days earlier than what the count implied. When Lindsay writes that *"points C and E are both effective"* he means they both point to tops but not the same top.

cases when points C and E are both effective [Figure 2.23].

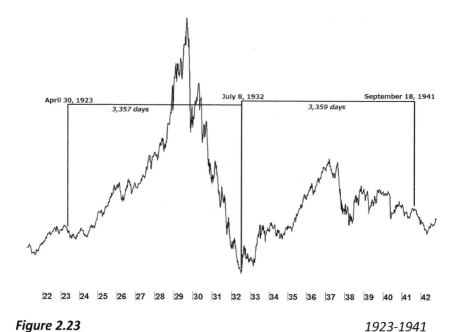

Figure 2.23   *1923-1941*

The bear market of 1917 was a link in one of the chains of equidistances. It was to indicate the time when another bear market would end. When counted from the last high of the multiple cycle in September 1929, points C and E both called for a low between February and May 1942.

The *"bear market of 1917"* began in November of 1916. Point C of the descending middle section was on December 12, 1916 and stretched for 4,648 days to the high in 1929 on September 3. Counting forward another 4,648 days from that high forecasts a low on May 26, 1942.

Point E of the bear market of 1917 was on March 20 of that year. The distance between then, and the bull market high in 1929, is 4,550 days. Counting forward another 4,550 days forecasts a low on February 17, 1942.

When Lindsay writes that the *"course of prices from 1937 to 1942 was typical of a terminal bear market"* he was referring to the fact that it was a long, drawn out bear market.

The course of prices from 1937 to 1942 was typical of a terminal bear market, such as that of 1890-1896. The low of a terminal decline is counted from the high of the same multiple cycle. An equidistance centered on March 1937 would therefore time the low more accurately than the count to 1917. Point E on January 14, 1932, was 1,882 days before the high of March 10, 1937. The low of April 28, 1942, was 1,875 days later [Figure 2.24].

Figure 2.24 *1932-1942*

The count can be made more precise by combining it with another principle. Certain intervals of time constantly recur. The most important is from 221 to 225 days. When this period has elapsed after the start of a movement, the trend either reverses or accelerates. If a count from a measuring point happens to expire at about the same time, the turn may be moved a few days so as to coincide with the 221-225 day limit.

For those readers acquainted with Lindsay's Three Peaks and a Domed House model, the time frame of 221 – 225 days may sound familiar. It has also become known as 7 months and 10 days. Lindsay used this time span to time the top of a bull market when using the 3PDh pattern. He also wrote that this interval shows up throughout the history of the Dow.

According to the rule of thumb, point E was January 14, 1932, the high day of the penultimate rally. But it could equally well have been January 21, 1932, since it can fall on any peak day in the same rally (paragraph 4, page 2) [Figure 2.25].

January 21, 1932, was 1,875 days before the high of March 10, 1937. The low of April 28, 1942, was exactly 1,875 days later. It was also 222 days after September 18, 1941, the last high day before one of the main waves of liquidation. April 28, 1942, was the only day that could have been precisely equidistant from either January 14 or 21, 1932, and, at the same time, between 221 and 225 days after September 18, 1941.

The same principle can be used to pinpoint many highs and lows, but must be applied with the time limit appropriate to the particular case. All counts in the Tables are given without adjustments.

When Lindsay writes of "adjustments" he is referring to the fact that the tables don't always reflect the standard time spans of basic advances and basic declines. In the tables he did not "adjust" for concepts such as secondary lows and sideways movements. Hence the counts in the tables do not always match the standard time spans. The counts are a simple accounting of the number of days involved in the basic cycles.

Figure 2.25: A ten-year forecast to the exact date!

Figure 2.25   *1932-1942*

Review Notes

When the low of a <u>terminal</u> bear market is to be counted, point J is the high of the same multiple cycle.

When the low of an <u>interior</u> bear market is to be found, point J is the high day of the final basic cycle in the previous long cycle.

To compute the date of the highest price in the second multiple cycle, an equidistance is taken from the longest ascending middle section available. If there was no ascending middle section of major proportions, the longest descending middle section is used. Point A must be the last low day of the multiple cycle in which the uptrend ended.

Highs and secondary lows are counted to long, ascending middle sections. Primary lows are equidistant from the shorter, descending middle sections.

Measuring points in a bear market may time both the highs and lows of the future but more often the lows. They may operate in either the basic or the major cycle, usually the latter.

Point C is the first drastically weak day in the main wave of liquidation which precedes the series of rallies.

An Aid to Timing

Chapter 3

3. An Aid to Timing

CALCULATION OF THE 1929 HIGH

The equidistances in Tables 1 and 2 show the basic cycle as it is after accommodations have been made so that it will agree with the major cycle. The basic cycle in unaltered form also leaves its impress on the price. The continuity cannot be detailed in limited space, but it is partially shown on the chart where the line changes from dotted to solid. The unaltered basic cycle retards the movement when it disagrees with the major cycle. But it controls the movement whenever there are measuring points in both cycles which permit it.

An "altered" basic cycle is composed of the advances and declines we all normally think of that stretch to market highs and lows. An altered cycle encapsulates the beginning and end of an advance or decline regardless of whether or not the basic movement (during the same time period) extended to the extreme that marked a turning point in the market.

When Lindsay writes of making "accommodations" he has in mind the "altered" basic cycle (and not the basic movements and their standard time spans). The basic movements and their standard time spans are "unaltered" and the basic cycles (which extend from ultimate lows to ultimate highs) are "altered". This is probably the opposite way most readers would think to label these concepts if unfamiliar with the basic movements.

The standard time spans don't always allow for a count to an absolute high or low and it is in these cases that concepts such as secondary lows and sideways movements come into play. See chapter five for a review of these concepts.

The basic cycle is shown at the bottom of many of the charts that follow.

"The unaltered basic cycle retards the movement when it disagrees with the major cycle". This was the case on June 10, 1940 shown in Figure 2.20 in chapter 2.

A basic cycle began at the low of March 30, 1926. The count must go back to a middle section in the 1923-1926 advance. That movement lacked a long, well defined middle section. Of its secondary middle sections, only one could give a count that would agree with the major cycle. It was between February and May 1924. Point C on February 15, 1924, was 774 days before the low of March 30, 1926. The high of May 15, 1928, was 775 days later [Figure 3.1].

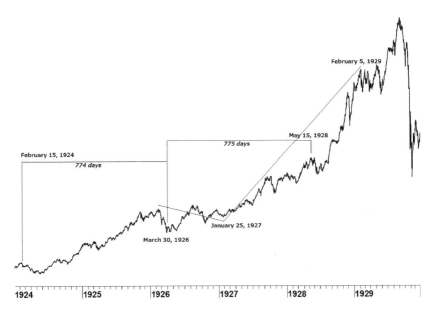

Figure 3.1   *1920s Middle Section and Basic Movements*

This is a good example of altered and unaltered basic cycles; the altered basic cycle begins on March 30, 1926. Elsewhere, Lindsay showed the time period between February 11, 1926 and January 25, 1927 as a sideways movement. Because of the sideways movement, the next basic advance (unaltered) after the 1926 high did not begin until January 25, 1927. See chapter 5 for a review of sideways movements.

The February to May middle section, in 1924, was a descending middle section rather than the typical ascending middle section Lindsay used to count to market tops. The change was made to make the count "agree with the major cycle".

The unaltered basic cycle, however, did not turn up until January 25, 1927. Since it remained in an uptrend until February 1929, the count that expired in May 1928 disagreed with it. A search must be made for a count that will support the unaltered basic cycle. If one can be found, it will be the correct measurement.

Here Lindsay is looking for a middle section that agrees with a basic advance between January 25, 1927 and February 5, 1929.

In later writings Lindsay described the advance between January 1927 and September 1929 as an extended basic advance (929 – 968 days) of 952 days. This made sense as his Principle of Alternation called for a long (or extended) advance off the January 1927 low because the previous advance (May 1920 – February 1926) had been a short basic advance. See chapter five for a review of the Principle of Alternation.

Note that all the counts examined here are contained within the long cycle of 1914-1932 and the multiple cycle of 1921-1932.

Since no middle section in the 1923-1926 advance could provide the count, it was necessary to go back to the period before the 1923 low. The 1921-1923 rise had a middle section which appeared between June and November 1922. It was disqualified because a count going back that far would cross two basic cycles [Figure 3.2].

Figure 3.2   *1922 Middle Section*

A major count demands a middle section
proportionately longer than those of the basic
cycle, if one is available. This requirement was
met by the middle section of the 1921-1926
advance (paragraph 7, page 4) [Chapter 1, Figure
1.24]. The measurement to this formation was thus
a major count which had to serve in finding the
high of the basic cycle.

A count from the low of March 1926 to point E in
January 1923 placed the top in June 1929. But the
high of February 11, 1926, was a turning point
equally as important as the low of March 30
[Figure 3.3]. It was 1,135 days after point E on
January 3, 1923. The low of March 26, 1929, was
1,139 days later. Such a count promises a rally
which will continue until it, in turn, becomes
equidistant from a measuring point.

Figure 3.3   *1923-1929 Middle Section Count*

A possible top in June
1929 conflicted with this
rally. It was therefore
necessary, when computing
the high, to carry the
count back to point C.

This forecast for a high
seven years later was off by
one day!

Point C on October 23, 1922, was 1254 days before
the low of March 30, 1926 [Figure 3.4]. The Dow-
Jones bull market high was 1,253 days afterward
on September 3, 1929.

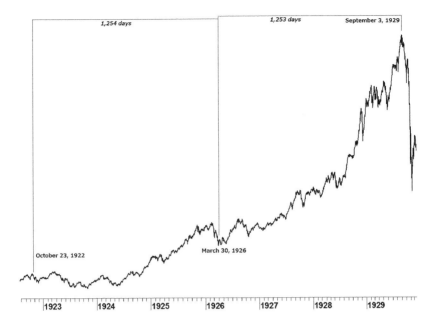

Figure 3.4   *Middle Section Count to September 3, 1929 high*

This date is now checked by finding a bearish equidistance centered on the low of March 26, 1929, which becomes a new point A. The uptrend from October 1927 to February 1929 was punctuated by two reactions, the first in May-June and the second in December 1928. They define an ascending middle section. The

Counting 176 days from the March 26, 1929 low over shoots the high in the Dow Industrials by 15 days.

Using another index (i.e. New York Times average) to justify a forecast made with the Dow Industrials was rare for Lindsay but it does appear at least one other time in his writings.

last rally was from November 1 to 28. The last rally but one was from October 3 to 24. The last rally but two ended in a line. October 1, 1928, was the last peak day in the line and became point E. It was 176 days before the low of March 26, 1929. The New York Times average made its bull market high 177 days later on September 19, 1929.

The middle section of 1899-1903 was described on page 4 [Chapter 1, Figure 1.22]. Point A was September 15, 1914. This last low of the multiple cycle was made on the curb while the stock exchange was closed. An equidistance from point E in February 1901 placed the high in April 1928. This conflicted with the count from 1926. The two ways of counting could be made to agree only by going back to point C on September 11, 1899. It was 5482 days before the low of September 15, 1914.

The outbreak of World War I in Europe forced the NYSE to shut its doors on July 31, 1914, after large numbers of foreign investors began selling their holdings in hopes of raising money for the war effort. Trading of stocks didn't resume until December 12, 1914. The American Stock Exchange was known as the Curb exchange at this time.

The New York Times high was 5483 days later on September 19, 1929. Since the count was to the longest ascending middle section, this date marked the high of the entire multiple cycle.

The low of March 1929 was measured by point E in January 1923. Point C in the same middle section was October 23, 1922. It was 1207 days before the high of February 11, 1926 [Figure 3.5]. The sustained rise began 1205 days later on May 31, 1929. This was another case when points C and E are both effective.

Figure 3.5   *Middle Section Count to May 1929 High*

There were three shifts in the computation. The first was from a short middle section in the basic cycle to a longer middle section. It was made to conform with two principles: 1. Highs are normally counted to long middle sections. 2. The unaltered basic cycle controls the movement whenever possible. The second shift was from point E to C, in order to avoid a conflict with another basic count.

The third was a shift from point E to C in the major cycle, so that it would coincide with the basic cycle.

> *"The unaltered basic cycle controls the movement whenever possible."* This statement provides an excellent tool to be used when searching for counts from middle sections. It can be interpreted to mean that, with very few exceptions, a middle section count needs to match a basic movement. When forecasting a high, a middle section count needs to point to a high which make sense when counting a basic advance (using the standard time spans) to the same high. The same guideline applies to declines.

A CHOICE OF MIDDLE SECTIONS

In the 1944-1946 advance, the chief middle section was from March to July 1945. The principle has been established that either reaction of an ascending middle section may constitute a separate descending middle section. It has most often been true of the second reaction. In the rail average, the second reaction, which began on June 27, became a descending middle section. The last rally was from July 27 to August 9. The last rally but one was from July 6 to 10. Point E was July 10, 1945, the high day of the penultimate rally. Point J was the bull market high in the rails, June 17, 1946. The price, however, was only five cents higher than on the previous business day, June 14, which was the true point J. It was 339 days after point E on July 10, 1945. The low of May 19, 1947, was 339 days later. This is an example of a shift from an ascending middle section to a shorter, descending middle section for the purpose of measuring a low. It is the most common type of shift.

In the industrial average, the corresponding decline could not constitute a middle section, because it had only one rally of consequence on the way down. But the period from December 1945 to February 1946 qualified as a middle section. Although ascending, it was short [Figure 3.6]. The first reaction was from December 10 to 21, 1945. The second reaction was from February 2 to 26, 1946. The last rally was from January 21 to February 2. The last rally but one was January 3 to 16. The last rally but two was from December 21 to 27. Point E on December 27, 1945, was 153 days before the bull market high in the industrial average, May 29, 1946. The low was 154 days afterward on October 30, 1946.

Figure 3.6   *Middle Section Count to October 1946 Low*

In this example Lindsay
identifies two middle sections
(one ascending, the other
descending) in the major cycle
and determines which is correct
by trying to match each of them
with a middle section taken
from the basic cycle.

Primary lows are often counted to the shorter, or
descending, middle section, when more than one
middle section appears in the same uptrend. The
lows of 1946 and 1947 followed the precedent. But
this was merely a probability. To determine which
middle section was correct, it was necessary to
consider how the two cycles would line up at the
turning points projected in the major cycle. The
major middle section of 1943 was described on
page 5 [Chapter 1, Figure 1.26]. A count from the
high of May 29, 1946, to point E on May 10, 1943,
called for a low on June 13, 1949 [Figure 3.7].
The second reaction, which began in July 1943,
formed a descending middle section [not shown].
Point E on September 20, 1943, placed the low on
February 4, 1949. The counts of the basic cycle
must now be balanced against this prospect.

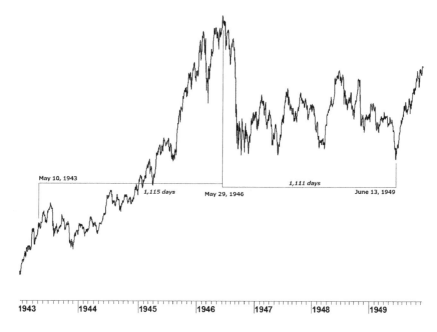

May 10, 1943

1,115 days

May 29, 1946

1,111 days

June 13, 1949

1943 1944 1945 1946 1947 1948 1949

Figure 3.7   *Middle Section Count to June 1949 Major Cycle Low*

If the low were counted from May 1946 to the long middle section of March–July 1945, it would fall in June 1947, twenty-five months after point E on May 7,

The major cycle shown in Figure 3.7 anticipates a low in June 1949. A high forecast by the basic cycle in July 1949 conflicts with the forecasted low by the major cycle.

"A high would then be scheduled for July 1949..." This comment is based on Lindsay's rule-of-thumb: two years up followed by one year down.

1945. It would necessarily become point A for the next advance. A high would then be scheduled for July 1949, fifty months after point E. Thus, a high in the basic cycle would almost coincide with a low in the major cycle. There would be a conflict [Figure 3.8].

123

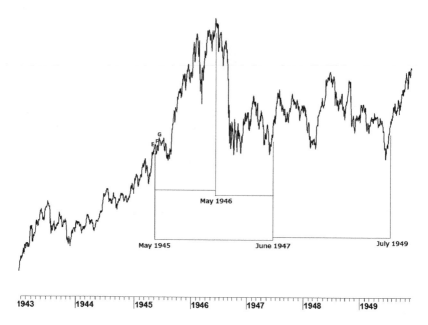

Figure 3.8   *1945 Middle Section Count*

If, on the other hand, the low were counted to point E in December 1945, in the short middle section, it would fall in October 1946 [Figure 3.9]. This date would become point A. Sufficient time would then remain for the basic cycle to advance and decline again, so that it would become even

Counting from point E in December 1945 to the market top in May 1946 was five months. Counting forward another five months targeted the low of October 1946.

A low in October 1946 could be followed by an advance of roughly two years and a decline of roughly one year placing a low in early 1949.

A short basic advance stretched 615 days from October 8, 1946 to the high of June 14, 1948. From that top enough time existed to fit in a short basic decline of 364 days to the June 13, 1949 low.

with the major cycle by 1949. There would be an
agreement. In deciding which middle section is
correct, it is always necessary to look ahead and
see how the two cycles will line up at all
turning points that can be projected.

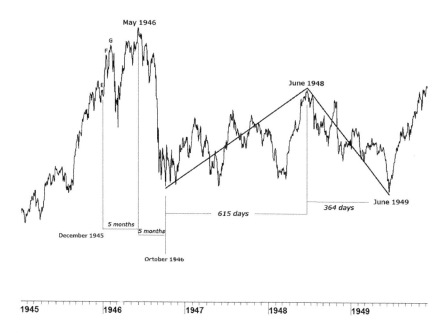

Figure 3.9   *1945-46 Middle Section Count and Basic Cycle*

It has been observed that the 1937-1942 decline
was a terminal bear market in form. On the
assumption that it was terminal, the declines of
1929-1932 and 1946 must be interior bear markets
[Figure 3.10]. The advance of 1938-1940 becomes
the last basic cycle in the previous long cycle.
The high of November 1938 acquires the force of
the highs listed in paragraph 2, page 12 [Chapter
2, Linked Equidistances, paragraph 1]. This
arrangement is the obverse of the pattern
described there.

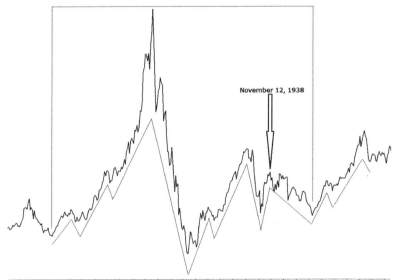

November 12, 1938

18 19 20 21 22 23 24 25 26 27 28 29 30 31 32 33 34 35 36 37 38 39 40 41 42 43 44 45 46 47 4

Figure 3.10   *1921-1942 Long Cycle*

> Important!
>
> Here Lindsay sets up a long cycle different from the long cycle he shows in Figure 2.1 in chapter 2.

According to the same principle which governs the chains of bear markets, a point E in the 1929-1932 decline should measure the low of 1946 or 1947 [Figure 3.11]. Actually, point E on November 25, 1930, was 2909 days before the high of November 12, 1938. The low of October 30, 1946, was 2909 days later. This count reaffirmed the choice of October 30, 1946, as point A, and therefore of December 27, 1945, as point E.

The November 1938 turning point is the high of the last basic cycle in the previous <u>multiple</u> cycle (not <u>long</u> cycle as was discussed in chapter 2, Linked Equidistances).

Having established the November 1938 high as the turning point *"From this high, the count goes back to point E (rarely C) in an interior bear market. The same number of days, when counted forward, arrives at or near the low of an interior bear market in the next long cycle."*

A perfect hit, 16 years later!

Figure 3.11   *1930 Middle Section Count to 1946 Low*

THE PRINCIPLE OF THE LOW

It has been seen that the low of 1949 was tentatively located before the low of 1946 was known. The ascending middle section of the major cycle placed it on June 19, 1949. The descending middle section called for the low on February 4.

In the basic cycle, point J was the high of June 14, 1948 [Figure 3.9]. Here, also, there was a second reaction which qualified as a descending middle section. It ran from July 1947 to February 1948. Point E could have been either October 20 or November 21, 1947. A count from June 14, 1948, to October 20, 1947, placed the low on February 7, 1949. Thus, equidistances from the descending middle sections of both the basic and the major cycles agreed on a low early in February 1949.

The ascending middle section of the basic cycle was described in paragraph 2, page 3 [Chapter 1, Ascending Middle Sections]. According to the rule of thumb, point E was June 23, 1947. But it could equally well have been June 16, since that was another peak day in the same rally. June 16, 1947, was 364

> Here Lindsay is forecasting the June 1949 low using a middle section from the <u>basic</u> cycle. It is also the low of a terminal bear market as shown in Figure 2.1. He is not concerned whether or not point J is the high of the same multiple cycle as he would if he were trying to forecast the low using a major cycle.

days before the high of June 14, 1948. The low of June 13, 1949, was exactly 364 days later. It was also 224 days after November 1, 1948, the last high day before one of the principal waves of liquidation. June 13, 1949, was the only day that could have been precisely equidistant from either June 16 or 23, 1947, and, at the same time, between 221 and 225 days after November 1, 1948.

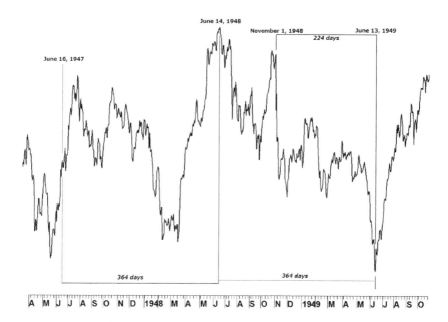

Figure 3.12   *June 1947 Middle Section Count to June 1949 low*

The ascending middle sections of both the basic and major cycles agreed on a bottom in June 1949, and June 13 was almost certainly the correct date. The remaining question was to decide whether the lowest price would occur then or in February as the two descending middle sections indicated. During the 1948-1949 period, there was no major equidistance from a previous severe decline, which would imply another sharp drop. In the absence of such a count, the measurement to 1933, which is given in Table 4, could be expected to support prices until it expires. The decline of 1948-1949 would therefore be mild.

The lows of the basic cycle are normally counted to the shorter, or descending, middle section. This is often, but not always, true, because the first rule is for the basic cycle to agree with the major cycle. But in the major cycle, the principle is invariable. The primary low of a severe decline is counted to a descending middle section. A secondary low is equidistant from an ascending middle section. The primary low of a decline that is mild compared to other similarly placed declines may be counted to an ascending middle section.

Typically, to determine the number of days from a turning point, to the low of a basic cycle, count backwards from the turning point to the measuring point in a descending middle section.

Always, to determine the number of days, from the turning point to the low in a major cycle, count backwards from the turning point to a descending middle section.

A secondary low is counted backward to an ascending middle section.

The low of a relatively mild decline may be counted backward to an ascending middle section.

If the decline held at the level of October 1946 [Figure 3.11], it would end at a secondary low from the long viewpoint. In that case, or if it were very mild, it must terminate in June 1949, when it would be counted to an ascending middle section. If a more severe drop had been in store, the low would have been indicated for February 1949.

October 1946 is only five months after the high of the basic advance which ended in May 1946. A "secondary low", as Lindsay would define it in later work, always occurs 13-14 months after the high of a bull market. Here he is using the term "secondary" in its generic sense. Regardless, he is making the point that a low in his counting system cannot end in October 1946 as it is too soon after the May 1946 market top.

The loss in 1912-1914 was small compared to other terminal bear markets. The count to point E on April 22, 1896, in Table 3, would have timed the low if the drop had been drastic. Actually, it measured only an intermediate fluctuation, because the multiple cycle turned up before then. The only other available middle section was ascending. Hence, the decline that ended in 1914 was mild for its position.

In the major cycle, the type of middle section regulates the degree of decline.

THE OLD AND THE NEW ALIGNMENTS

An interior bear market has only brief rallies prior to its lowest point. But a terminal decline has one or more rallies that embrace an entire basic cycle [Figure 2.1]. There have been four interior declines in every long cycle, although the last of the series may form the first leg of the terminal bear market, as in 1890. For more than a century, the same sequence of interior and terminal declines was unbroken.

The drop of 1929-1932 occupied the position of a terminal bear market [Figure 2.1]. But in structure and in major equidistance, it was interior. Since it was required to be severe (for a reason which belongs to another phase of the subject), the count had to go back to a descending middle section. According to paragraph 2, page 12, [Chapter 2, Linked Equidistances], the low of a terminal decline must be counted from the high of the same multiple cycle - in this case, September 1929. Because of the extraordinary rise from 1921 onward, there was no possible descending middle section which could be used.

"But in structure and in major equidistance, it was interior." The 1929-1932 decline did not have *"...one or more rallies that embrace an entire basic cycle. "* That is to say, it contained no rally which could be counted as a basic advance (see chapter five for more on the basic movements).

The drop of 1929-1932 was *"required to be severe"* because, as Lindsay noted elsewhere, all declines following an advance out of a sideways movement are always severe. Sideways movements are typically topping formations. But in 1927 the Dow advanced, rather than dropped, from the sideways movement between February 1926 and January 1927.

September 1929 was the high of the same multiple cycle (point J). Lindsay was searching for a descending middle section to count backwards to from there.

The equidistance had to be centered on another turning point. The low of July 8, 1932, was 4631 days after the high of November 3, 1919 [Figure 3.13]. Point C on February 25, 1907, was 4634 days earlier (a count to point E would not have agreed with the basic cycle). This was the only available measurement to a major descending middle section. Since point J in November 1919 was, not in the same, but in the previous multiple cycle [Figure 2.1], the decline was necessarily interior.

In this example Lindsay is timing the low of the great bear market of 1929-1932. He was forced to use a different turning point (November 3, 1919) than his rules and the long cycle suggest due to the lack of a descending middle section during the bull market of the 1920s.

Lindsay's comment *"a count to point E would not have agreed with the basic cycle"* refers to the fact that the count from point E on July 8, 1907 (the last day in a "line") to the high of November 3, 1919 is 4,501 days. Counting forward another 4,501days targets a low on February 29, 1932. Lindsay counted the bear market of 1929-1932 as two basic declines which began, not at the high in 1929, but from the right shoulder/end of the sideways movement on April 17, 1930. The first decline was a long basic decline of 411 days which terminated on June 2, 1931. After a quick bounce, the second basic decline began on June 27, 1931 and terminated after another long basic decline of 376 days on July 8, 1932. Counting from the 1931 high to a low on February 29, 1932 would have been a subnormal decline of only 247 days.

A miss of three days over a period of more than 25 years!

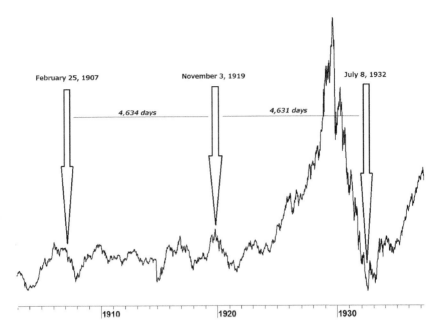

Figure 3.13   *1907 Middle Section Count to July 1938 Low*

The next downtrend in 1934 was also interior. There were now four successive interior declines in two multiple cycles 1923, 1926, 1932 and 1934 [Figure 3.14]. The following bear market must be terminal. Actually, the 1937-1942 drop had terminal characteristics. The overall pattern was the same as if a long cycle had begun in 1921 and ended in 1942.

|21 |22 |23 |24 |25 |26 |27 |28 |29 |30 |31 |32 |33 |34 |35 |36 |37 |38 |39 |40 |41 |42 |

Figure 3.14   *Four successive declines*

This arrangement crisscrosses the old progression of interior and terminal bear markets. It instituted a new alignment. It has established a fourth chain of interior declines: 1907 to 1932 to 1946. If it continues, the result will be a long cycle beginning in 1942 and ending about 1961. The 1949 low, however, was derived from the old order [Figure 2.1].

At the unusual double bottom of 1946 and 1949, the two influences were evenly balanced. But one of them will predominate in the future.

The Dow Industrials never did print a new low after the publication of Lindsay's paper in March 1950 and exceeded the 1946 high only one month later.

If the old arrangement should prevail, the terminal decline of 1946-1949 would be resumed. Prices would recede before they equal the top level of 1946. The high would be timed by one of the first two incomplete counts in Table 4. The final low would be counted from the high of the same multiple cycle, May 1946, to point E in January 1941. The count is included in Table 3.

The count from December 9, 1933 (fourth from the bottom in table four) counts 3,062 days to point A on April 28, 1942. Lindsay left this count unfinished as it counts to a high in September 1950, nine months after he published his paper, _An Aid to Timing_.

The two incomplete counts Lindsay refers to here count to highs in September 1950 and February 1951. The Dow did see a top on February 13, 1951 followed by a very brief correction.

Another long cycle would then begin. Under the new alignment, however, these counts may measure intermediate movements.

The third incomplete count in Table 2 counts to a high on September 20, 1951. The actual high came seven days earlier, on September 13, 1951. It functions as the top of a long basic advance of 822 days from the low of June 13, 1949. This high is examined, in detail, in chapter six.

On the premise that the new progression has gained the upper hand, one of the incomplete counts in Table 2 will measure the high of the current advance. There are five guides in selecting the right date:

1. The two cycles agree when they both have measuring points which permit it.
2. Highs are normally counted to long, ascending middle sections.
3. Another equidistance may conflict with one of the alternative dates.
4. When all the middle sections of the advance are clear, an estimate can be made of how the next decline will fit in with the major count.
5. When the total advance in a basic cycle lasts less than two years, the deepest reaction starts before the end of the first year. When the advance lasts more than two years, a sell-off deeper than any previous one occurs during the second year. This has been true in 21 of 26 cases. Two of the exceptions could be interpreted both ways.

In the event that the five indicators point to two different dates, as seems likely in the present instance, both of them will probably be correct to some degree, although only one, of course, can mark the highest price.

An interior decline will follow. The equidistance centered on the last high of the previous long cycle, November 12, 1938, in Table 3, gives the latest date when the downtrend can reverse. Since the count goes to an ascending middle section, it may measure a secondary low, and the loss will not be drastic. Under these conditions, a trading market is probable during the interval between the high of the current advance and the next strong upthrust in 1953. The pattern will emerge as the measuring points of the basic cycle become known.

> The count from November 1938 (shown in Table 3) extends to February 1953. Lindsay wrote that this count should find a market low. A minor low, followed by a month-long advance was printed on February 20, 1953. As it turned out, the advance off the June 1949 low was followed by a Three Peaks and Domed House formation which did not peak until January 5, 1953. But the following decline did not bottom until September 1953.
>
> The "*next strong upthrust in 1953*" began at the September low and saw the market advance over 200% during the next 2 ½ years.

Another terminal decline will not begin until the expiration of the last incomplete count in Table 4. It will be noted that a severe bear market in the next five years is possible only as a continuation of the decline from 1946. Once the downtrend is broken, there will be no count to a major descending middle section until 1955.

The count from October 30, 1946, in Table 4, will be the first important bearish equidistance to expire since the

> The count from October 30, 1946 did not produce a high.
>
> The advance Lindsay expected in the summer of 1950 began on July 13.

main trend turned up in June 1949. If the old multiple cycle still prevails, a sharp sell-off will follow. It will go deeper than an ordinary technical reaction. Under the new alignment, however, this count should not have a pronounced effect on prices. Thus, the character of the decline will furnish additional evidence on the status of the two alignments. In either event, the sell-off will be temporary, as an advance is indicated for the summer of 1950.

Not every possible count is listed in the Tables. The available space has limited the discussion to those principles and equidistances that seem most important. Many points, including short term movements, have necessarily been passed over.

Written March 15, 1950

Review Notes

Either reaction of an ascending middle section may unfold as a descending middle section but it has most often occurred in the second reaction.

Highs are normally counted to long middle sections.

In the major cycle, the type of middle section regulates the degree of decline.

The low of a terminal decline must be counted from the high of the same multiple cycle.

Primary lows are often counted to the shorter, or descending, middle section, when more than one middle section appears in the same uptrend.

The lows of the basic cycle are normally counted to the shorter, or descending, middle section. This is often, but not always, true, because the first rule is for the basic cycle to agree with the major cycle. But in the major cycle, the principle is invariable.

The primary low of a severe decline is counted to a descending middle section.

A secondary low is equidistant from an ascending middle section.

Review Notes

The primary low of a decline that is mild compared to other similarly placed declines may be counted to an ascending middle section.

The first rule is for the basic cycle to agree with the major cycle.

A major count demands a middle section proportionately longer than those of the basic cycle.

In the major cycle, the type of middle section regulates the degree of decline.

The unaltered basic cycle controls the movement whenever possible.

When all the middle sections of the advance are clear, an estimate can be made of how the next decline will fit in with the major count.

When the total advance in a basic cycle lasts less than two years, the deepest reaction starts before the end of the first year. When the advance lasts more than two years, a sell-off deeper than any previous one occurs during the second year.

22 year Overlay
Chapter 4

Ed Carlson

4. 22-year Overlay

"The purpose of this long-term method is only partly to learn the time of the high – although the method tells us this with fair accuracy in many cases, as anyone can see who figures out each interval from a more detailed chart. The chief purpose of the method is to estimate, long ahead of time, whether the decline that follows the Moment of Truth will be a drastic bear market, or simply a run-of-the-mill setback." - George Lindsay

Don't skip over the opening quote too quickly. While forecasting the timing of highs and lows is important, that information can be had from Lindsay's other methods (*"...as anyone can see who figures out each interval from a more detailed chart"*). This chapter seeks to showcase Lindsay's method for estimating the <u>intensity</u> of a correction following a projected market high or *Moment of Truth*. When Lindsay writes of a 'run-of-the-mill setback' he is referring to any pullback up to, and including what most market participants think of as a bear market ; a 20% decline. A "significant" market decline to Lindsay was one approximating 40% or more. Hence, this chapter teaches how to distinguish forecasts for typical bear markets from true wealth-destroying, career-ending market declines.

The reader, who wants to forecast a turn in the market to the exact day, or within a very small range of days, will need to be acquainted with the standard time spans and counts from the middle section.

Lindsay's standard approach for forecasting a market top was to start with the 15year interval. This is an interval, counted from an important low, which normally extends anywhere from 15years to 15years and 11 months. It is within this 11-month time frame that Lindsay then applied his standard time spans and counts from the middle section to narrow down his forecast for an exact point-estimate of a top. To find market bottoms Lindsay used a 12year interval; an interval counted from an important high to a time frame 12years, 2months to 12years, 8months later. It is within this time frame that

Lindsay applied the same methods to pinpoint a market bottom. Lindsay used the 22 year overlay explained in this chapter to place that 15year interval into context and estimate the intensity of the coming decline. No similar overlay for 12year intervals has been found.

Finding the origin of a 15 or 12 year interval by itself isn't terribly difficult. It is similar to identifying the low of a Separating Decline in the Three Peaks and a Domed House pattern. An important low is typically a market low which has breached a low prior to the intervening high (Figure 4.1). It may also be the low of a sustained advance out of a market consolidation but that isn't as common. Lindsay wrote that he was able to trace these intervals back to 1802. To do this he used the book *"Fluctuations in American Business 1790-1860."* He then created his own index for the years until the Dow Jones Industrial index was created.

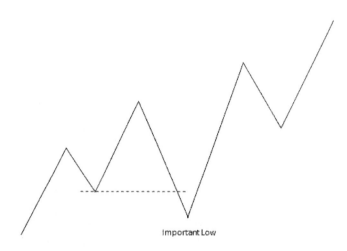

Important Low

Figure 4.1   *Important Low (generic)*

In the 22 year overlay we are searching for three important intervals ending at a high 22 years, 15 years, and 8 years later. Lows appear approximately every 7 years followed by a high (the Moment of Truth) 8 years later after the final low.

The 22year interval is not so important in deciding the exact time of the high at the Moment of Truth. But unless a major low falls there, a really severe decline is unlikely following the Moment of Truth 22 years later.

The 15year interval is the most important of the three. Unless a first-class low falls on 15 year date, a long or severe bear market is very unlikely to begin at the Moment of Truth.

The 8year interval is usually important from the standpoint of determining the time of the high, but it has little influence on the depth of the following decline. The 8 year line by itself never indicates a major decline after the Moment of Truth. It is not necessary for the 8 year low to be a major low in order to give a bearish forecast. The declines in 1919-1921(-46.6%) and in 1937-1942 (-49%) both had lows of no importance at the 8 year interval.

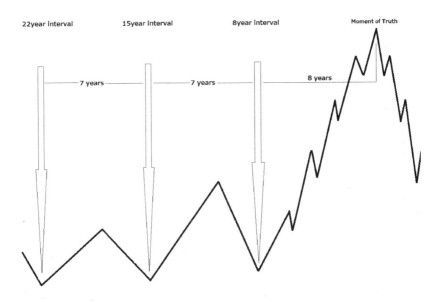

Figure 4.2   *22 year overlay, Typical Scheme*

Normally one major bear market holds above the nadir of the previous one. There have been only a limited number of exceptions to this rule. On these few occasions, the length of the most important interval has been modified and has come closer to 16 years (i.e. 15years, 11months) instead of the usual 15 years. The breached low must be a significant low and the later this breach occurs in the overlay (i.e. after the eight year interval) the less important it becomes. The breach may occur by an "interval low" undercutting another "interval low". It may be an "interval low" undercutting a "non-interval low". It may even be the result of a "non-interval low" undercutting a prior "interval low". The important point to remember is that the low which is breached must be of some significance regardless of where it lies in the overlay pattern.

As shown in the following examples, when the 15 year interval is increased by one year to create a 16 year interval, the distance between the 22 and 16 year lines becomes closer to six years than to seven. Sometimes the market adjusts the interval to become seven years apart and sometimes not. How to handle this becomes clear with practice and is shown in the examples that follow. When the opposite situation occurs and the seven year interval becomes closer to eight years, this reduces the expected level of bearishness of the eventual decline.

It has been your author's observation that these 22year overlays are often followed by a formation Lindsay called *Three Peaks and a Domed House.* The top of the Domed House often occurs approximately three to four years after the Moment of Truth.

1907-1929

Figure 4.3 shows the most bearish possible pattern – when a major low falls on each of the intervals – and the greatest decline in history followed, on September 3, 1929. Using his pre-Dow data, Lindsay wrote that the bull market high of 1881 was also timed by three lows of the very first magnitude, although they did not come exactly seven years apart. Stocks then declined from 1881 until 1896, a downtrend lasting fifteen years.

Two Three Peaks/Domed House patterns occur after the 1929 top. The cupola of the first pattern was on February 5, 1934 – 4years and 5months later – and the cupola of the second formation appeared on March 10, 1937 – 7years and 6months later.

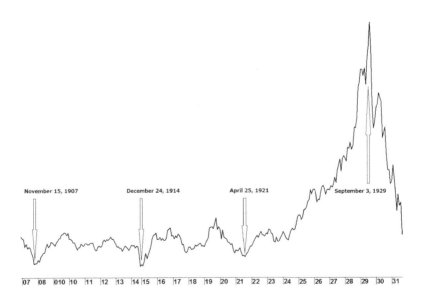

Figure 4.3   *1907-1929*

1914-1937

In Figure 4.4, we see that lows of the first magnitude fell on the 22 and 15 year junctures. But there was only a minor low at the 8 year interval. This is the second most bearish pattern. The Dow made a high on March 10, 1937, fifteen and a half years after the low of August 24, 1921, and then dropped by more than 50% before the bear market was over.

The 1937 high should have been 16 years, rather than 15, since the bottom of 1932 was lower than that of 1921. It was about 2 weeks closer to 16 years, than 15, but more importantly, if the interval is counted to the secondary peak of August 13, 1937 just before the big plunge, the interval is almost exactly 16 years. As the 1932 low was late in the pattern (after the eight year interval) the indecision by the market whether to extend the 15 year interval to 16 years makes sense.

This 22year overlay was followed by a rare inversion of the Three Peaks/Domed House pattern; a domed house followed by three peaks. The third peak on April 6, 1940 was almost exactly three years after the 1937 Moment of Truth.

Figure 4.4   *1914-1937*

1903-1926

In Figure 4.5, a major low fell at the 22year point. The low of 1917, at the 8year line, was of only slightly less than the first importance. But the low of 1910, at the 15 year mark, was only a second-grade bottom. Therefore, when the market arrived at the Moment of Truth on February 11, 1926 the following break was of short-term significance only. The price action in 1926 shows the importance of the 15year interval.

The Moment of Truth in February 1926 was followed by a Three Peaks/Domed House and the top of its cupola was printed on September 3, 1929 – 3years and 6months after the Moment of Truth.

Figure 4.5   *1903-1926*

1896 - 1919

The 22 and 15year intervals (1896 and 1903) both fell at important lows in the Dow index and were seven years apart (Figure 4.6). The 8year interval in 1911 was not an important low but 8year intervals are used to help time the Moment of Truth and not to determine the intensity of the following decline. The Moment of Truth appeared to have been set up for a severe decline and it did not disappoint. The November high in 1919 was followed by a 44% decline in the equity index.

The November 1919 high was followed by a Three Peaks/Domed House and the top of its cupola, March 19, 1923, was 3years and 4months after the Moment of Truth.

Figure 4.6   *1896-1919*

1917 - 1940

In the 22 year interval from 1917 to 1940, the low of 1932 breached the previous low in 1923. This told us to expect a 16 year interval instead of the usual 15 years (Figure 4.7).

The high of September 13, 1939, fell very close to the indicated times: nearly 22 years after the 1917 bottom and 16 years after the 1923 low. But prices did nothing worse than sag for the next eight months, and this shows the importance of the eight year interval as a factor in timing. There would be a high eight years after the major low of July 8, 1932, which would place it in the summer of 1940. When the various intervals expire several months apart, as in 1939-1940, there is a tendency for prices to decline after the end of the first interval. But stocks seldom fall precipitously at that point; they hold fairly close to the earlier high until the expiration of the last interval of the series. However, the market has seldom held up longer than six or eight months for this purpose. When the discrepancy between two intervals is greater than that, prices have usually broken sharply after the first one. They then recovered later and made a new top formation at the time the last interval in the series expired.

Figure 4.7

1917-1940

1926 - 1948

The 15 year interval from 1932 becomes 16 years because the bottom of 1942 was below the lows of 1938 and 1940 (Figure 4.8). The breach in this case occurred late in the overlay and led to an insignificant correction after the Moment of Truth. Calling March 30, 1926 the 22 year point made the interval closer to 6 years than 7 but at 6 years and 3 months it was still closer to 7 years than a count to the next obvious low of May 29, 1924 (8 years, 1 month). The low of June 10, 1940 came at exactly the 8 year point but it was a secondary bottom; a bottom of no significance. The appearance of a top on June 14, 1948 was excellent timing and met expectations for a mild 'bear market'; no more than a correction in this instance. If a major bear market low had occurred in 1926 at the 22 year point, then we would have expected a severe drop in 1948-1949, after the Moment of Truth.

The Moment of Truth in June 1948 was followed by a Three Peaks/Domed House which saw its high printed on January 5, 1953 – 4years and 6months after the Moment of Truth.

Figure 4.8   *1926-1948*

1930 - 1953

The high of January 5, 1953 was within three months of 15 years from the important low of March 31, 1938. And the secondary high of March 17, 1953 would have made it exactly so. But with only a minor low at the 8 year point and no real low at the 22 year point, the bear market following the 1953 high was destined to be only moderate in scope (Figure 4.9).

The 1953 "top" was followed by a Three Peaks/Domed House in 1955-1956. The top of the formation was printed 3years, 3months after the Moment of Truth in 1953.

Figure 4.9   *1930-1953*

1932 - 1954

The elements for a high in 1954 never quite fit together the way they should have. The bottom of 1942 was below the bottom in 1938 (Figure 4.10). That tells us that the important high should be 16 years after the low in 1938, not 15 years. In this new scenario the important low of 1946 falls at the 8 year point. With the intervals falling on important lows things were shaping up for a very dramatic decline, the most severe since 1929. However, there are two things wrong with this picture:

The 1938 (16 year) low no longer "fits" into our picture. March 31, 1938 is less than 5 years and 9 months after the important low of July 8, 1932 – which is a heartbreakingly perfect 22 years prior to the 1954 high. The 15/16 year low should come seven years after the 22 year low. This is a prerequisite for a deep decline after the Moment of Truth.

The second and more compelling problem is that the 15/16 year interval is the most important of the three intervals and a decline must begin either 15 or 16 years after every important low; but never after both. Since a well-defined and extended downtrend began at the exact 15year interval in 1953, it was very unlikely that a new decline, even more severe, would begin a year later in 1954.

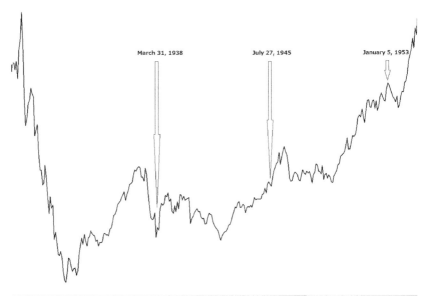

Figure 4.10   *1932-1954*

1932 - 1957

The lows of April 28, 1942 and June 13, 1949 fit very nicely as 15 and 8 year intervals. They called for a top in 1957 (Figure 4.11). When two important counts so nearly coincide, the outcome is highly probable and a moderate decline did get underway on July 12, 1957. But with no important low 22 years prior to 1957(the 1932 low was 25 years prior) the sell-off was destined to be mild. The total loss was about 20%.

The 1957 Moment of Truth was followed by a Three Peaks/Domed House formation which topped 4years and 5months later on December 13, 1961.

Figure 4.11   *1932-1957*

1939 - 1961

The period from 1939 to 1961 is similar to the previous example. Important lows, 7 years apart, are spotted in October 1946 and September 1953 (Figure 4.12). Two important lows set apart as these two are indicate a top 15 and 8 years later, respectively, in 1961. But, like the previous example, no important low exists 22 years prior to 1961 in 1939. A minor low in 1939 can be counted 22 years forward to the 1961 high but a major low is required for a bear market of the first magnitude. The significant low of 1938 was 8 years and 7 months before the 15year low of October 1946; too long to fit Lindsay's model. The forecast then was for a respectable pullback in 1961. The total loss that year was about 37%.

The 1961 Moment of Truth was followed by a Three Peaks/Domed House formation in 1964-1966. The top of the formation was on February 9, 1966, 4years and 3months after the Moment of Truth.

Figure 4.12   *1939-1961*

1942 - 1966

"In the years between the decline of 1937-1938 and the present moment [1964], these long-term intervals have never once shown the kind of setup that normally precedes a major bear market. Never before in history had a quarter of a century passed without at least one drastic market decline. It was against all experience to suppose that it would ever happen. Yet these long-term intervals indicated that there would be no break of the first magnitude in all that time. I do not know of any other technical method which suggested, even indirectly, that there would be no major decline in all those 26 years."

At the time Lindsay wrote of these intervals in 1964 he could not see its end yet. At that time he expected the Moment of Truth to arrive in the spring of that year but allowed for the possibility that the final high might not occur until 1966. That suspicion was based on the interplay of medium term intervals (the standard time spans).

"According to precedent, a major decline should begin within a few months." While the 8 year interval (May 25, 1956)fell at a low of no significance, the 22 and 15 year intervals are the two most important points and they did fall at important lows (April 28, 1942 and June 13, 1949); hence, his call for a "major decline".

Lindsay noticed that the low of June 26, 1962 had breached the previous low of October 25, 1960 but argued against moving to a 16 year interval as his rule for this concerns one low breaking under a previous bottom of *major importance*. He concluded the low of 1960 was not a low of major importance therefore he felt that using a 15 year interval had the highest probability of success in this case. He was also bothered by the fact that the lows in question came so late in the sequence unlike other examples in which this trigger for a 16 year interval came earlier. He did mention the possibility of counting the 8 year interval from the October 22, 1957 low – clearly an important low. That point counts a very nice 8 years, 3 months to the February 1966 high (Figure 4.13).

Using Lindsay's rule that the 15 year interval becomes 16 years when one low undercuts a previous low moves the forecasted high from late 1964 to late 1965. The high arrived on February 9, 1966; almost 16 years and 8 months after the 15/16 year point. A final bottom was not seen until four years later on 5/26/1970. By that time the Dow had lost over 36% from its 1966 high versus an expected +45% drop if it had begun at the exact 22 and 15 year intervals.

The February 1966 Moment of Truth was followed by a Three Peaks/Domed House formation which topped 2years and almost 10months later on December 3, 1968.

Figure 4.13   *1942-1966*

1946 - 1968

Lindsay labels the low of October 9, 1946 an important low but refers to the September 14, 1953 low as "not of major scope". He concludes, therefore, that the forecasted decline of 1968 will be relatively mild.

Interestingly, he writes *"It may become important if there is a bear market already in progress at the time, and the long-term intervals shown in Chart 15* [Figure 4.14] *simply result in a prolongation of it."* The high of 1968 is probably best described as a double-top with the first top being the February 1966 top discussed previously. The 1968 high (985.21) was just below the February 1966 high (995.15) making the decline following December 1968 high a "prolongation" of the post-1966 bear market. Also of interest is that his expectation of a 15year interval, rather than 16 years (despite the 1962 breach of the 1960 low) works better here than in the previous example.

Figure 4.14   *1946-1968*

1949 - 1973

Lindsay calls both the 1949 and 1957 lows important and therefore a very bearish setup (Figure 4.15). But he notes that the two lows, June 13, 1949 and October 22, 1957, are 8 years apart which reduces the expected level of bearishness of the eventual decline. That decline (-45%) in 1973 didn't occur until 15 years after the 15year point in 1957 and 23 years after the 1949 low. In this case, there was no attractive candidate for the 8year interval. The closest low is June 28, 1965 which would make the 8 year interval two months shorter than the previous 7 year interval from 1957 (7 years, 6 months versus 7 years, 8 months).

The January 1973 Moment of Truth was followed by an odd Three Peaks/Domed House formation in which the three peaks were part of the decline following the 1973 top. The high of the cupola was seen on September 21, 1976, 3years and 8months after the Moment of Truth.

Figure 4.15   *1949-1973*

1953 - 1976

In Figure 4.16 Lindsay noted that the lows of 1953 and 1960 fall exactly as they should, 7 years apart. This should result in some sort of decline at the Moment of Truth in 1975 but because neither low was important, the loss was expected to be relatively small. What Lindsay couldn't see when he wrote his comments in 1964 were the breached lows in the years to come. This would have told him to expect a 23 year interval to the final high, not 22 years.

The high in September 1976 was almost exactly 23 years after the low in September 1953 and 15 years, 10 months after the October 1960 low. The market fell 26% after that high.

The high of a Three Peaks/Domed House formation was on April 27, 1981 – 4years and 7months after the Moment of Truth on September 21, 1976.

September 14, 1953   October 25, 1960   March 21, 1968   September 21, 1976

Figure 4.16   *1953-1976*

"The long-term intervals are a method of timing market tops. They are no more accurate in doing this than a number of other approaches are. Their chief advantage is that they tell us what they have to say much sooner than any other technique does. To derive any benefit from them, you must know how to capitalize on this one clear point of superiority."

"Can you rely on the method? It is certainly not infallible. It is certainly possible to miscalculate the intervals. And the technique will not necessarily work as well in the future as it did in the past. Furthermore, it cannot be applied to speculative stocks: it must be used only with issues of investment merit. At worst, however, it is a systematic and considered way of doing something that nearly everyone does haphazardly. At one time or another, you must decide either to dump your stocks or to sweat them out, as the case may be. A knowledge of the long-term intervals might help you make the decision more intelligently than you would otherwise."

George Lindsay

Review Notes

The 22 year overlay is used to find three important intervals ending at the same high: 22years, 15years, and 8years. Lows appear approximately every 7 years followed by a high (the Moment of Truth) 8 years later.

The 22 year interval must be a major low; otherwise a severe decline is unlikely following the Moment of Truth 22 years later.

The 15 year interval is the most important of the three. Unless a first-class low falls on 15 year date, a long or severe bear market is very unlikely to begin at the Moment of Truth.

The 8year interval is important from the standpoint of determining the time of the high, but it has little influence on the depth of the following decline. It is not necessary for the 8 year low to be a major low in order to give a bearish forecast.

Normally one major bear market holds above the nadir of the previous one. When a previous low has been breached, the length of the most important interval has been modified and has come closer to 16 years instead of the usual 15. The later this breach occurs in the overlay (i.e. after the eight year interval) the less important it becomes. The low which is breached must be of some significance regardless of where it lies in the overlay pattern.

Long-term Intervals

And Basic Movements

Chapter 5

Ed Carlson

5. Long-term Intervals and Basic Movements

Lindsay's work is often incorrectly described as cycles. It is not. Although the information contained in the first three chapters of this book does deal with cycles, most people have never had the opportunity to read that material. The work that most people are acquainted with is what he called "intervals". Rather than counting these intervals from a theoretical high or low, as one might when using actual cycles, he counted from the actual highs and lows seen in the market. Anyone using the cycles described in earlier chapters will want to narrow down the time spans in which to search for the forecasted high or low. This is accomplished by beginning with the long-term intervals to find a multi-month time frame. This time period is expected to contain the market inflection point and can be narrowed even further using Lindsay's basic movements. Once these two exercises are completed, the analyst can then attempt a more precise forecast using Lindsay's model of counting from middle sections.

This chapter also includes a review of Lindsay's two most important principles; the Principle of Continuity and the Principle of Alternation. Both principles are simple, yet important, guidelines. The Principle of Continuity prevents the analyst from becoming distracted by the temptation of seemingly attractive, but false counts. The Principle of Alternation provides a foothold for an initial attempt at identifying a basic movement.

The chapter concludes with two final concepts; Secondary Lows and Sideways Movements. Secondary Lows are an integral part of Lindsay's method and differentiate it from all other market-timing models. This very simple concept, combined with the Principle of Continuity, is where the "magic" of Lindsay is revealed. Sideways Movements, while rare, are akin to the error term in a linear regression equation. When a long-term interval and basic movement fail to connect as they should, this concept keeps the analyst on track until

Lindsay's short-term methods can be used to identify a market high.

Long-term Intervals

A long-term interval is the elapsed time from an important low to an important high or vice versa. Bull market highs are counted from an important low to an important high and the interval is referred to as a 15year interval. Bear market bottoms are counted from an important high to an important low and are called 12year intervals.

The long-term intervals are not used to forecast the exact "address" of a market inflection point. Rather, they should be thought of as forecasting the exact "zip code". The long-term interval from an important low targets an important high anywhere between 15years and 15years, 11months later; an 11month time frame in which to start the search for a market high. Market tops are most commonly found in the time span of 15years 2months – 4months (Figure 5.1). When searching for a market low, the search takes place in a 6month time frame which extends anywhere from 12years, 2months to 12years, 8months from an important high(Figure 5.2).

Figure 5.1   *15year interval 1957-1973*

Figure 5.2   *12year interval 1929-1942*

These long-term intervals are not to be confused with trends (Figures 5.2 and 5.3). These highs and lows should not be thought of as highs and lows in relation to each other. They are localized highs and lows; i.e. a high is determined to be a high relative to the other highs near it and not to a low 15years in the past. The same principle holds for lows. Lindsay made clear that the trend during the time span of an interval is unimportant. A low may count to a high which is lower than the original low. A high may count to a low which is higher than the original high (Figure 5.4).

March 1937

August 1921

1920 |1921 |1922 |1923 |1924 |1925 |1926 |1927 |1928 |1929 |1930 |1931 |1932 |1933 |1934 |1935 |1936 |1937 |1938 |1939 |1

Figure 5.3   *15year interval, 1921-1937*

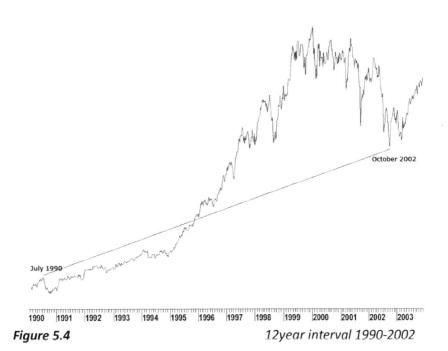

Figure 5.4   *12year interval 1990-2002*

Basic Movements

A long-term interval provides a target range of dates but that range is very broad. To narrow down the time span in which the high or low is expected, we compare the long-term intervals with, what Lindsay called, the medium-term counts or basic movements. These two classes of counts must be combined in order to make a forecast. When the end of a basic movement and the end of a long-term interval coincide in time, there is a decisive movement in the market. In Figure 5.5 a long-term interval can be counted between the low of September 14, 1953 to 15years and 2months later on December 3, 1968. The December high is also counted as a long basic advance of 788 days from the low on October 7, 1966.

Figure 5.5   *15year interval and basic advance 1953-1968*

The simplest possible generalization of the basic movements is that stock prices rise for approximately two years, decline for about a year, then rise for another two year span and drop for a year. And so on indefinitely. Lindsay used the term "basic" to distinguish the advances and declines derived from his methods from generic advances and declines in the market. Generic advances and declines are the "adjusted" advances and declines referred to in earlier chapters which comprise the basic cycles. The basic or "unadjusted" advances and declines are counted using the standard time spans.

The great gift or insight Lindsay left to the rest of us was his recognition and categorization of the standard time spans. Lindsay wrote that all advances and declines tend to cluster together into groups of similar duration. He called these groups the standard time spans. They are the number of days which comprise the different basic movements; basic advances and basic declines. Lindsay always used calendar days, not trading days, in his work. The different basic advances and declines and their standard time spans are listed in Table 5.1.

Standard Time Spans

	Advances	Declines
Subnormal	**414-615**	**222-250**
Short	**630-718**	**317-364**
Long	**742-830**	**376-446**

Table 5.1   *Standard Time Spans*

In addition to counting the basic advances and declines from the end of the previous basic decline or advance (per the Principle of Continuity) Lindsay also specified that the basic movements can be counted from any "important" high or low – *"the highs and lows that jump off the page at you"*. Figure 5.6 illustrates an important low. An important low breaches the low of an earlier decline in a previous uptrend.

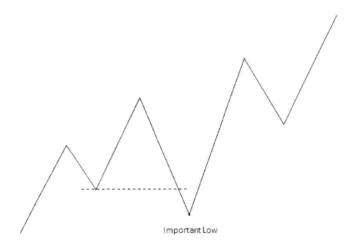

Figure 5.6   *Important Low*

Lindsay referred to these time spans as "standard" because they have occurred over and over again throughout history (since 1790) and each span only varies within the narrow limits shown. I refer to the time period between the spans as "no man's land". For example, in Lindsay's counting method there has never been an advance lasting 900 days because that duration is too long for a long basic advance (742-830 days) and too short for an extended basic advance (929-968 days). Remembering this can give the analyst an edge in trying to eliminate possible counts from a forecast.

Principle of Continuity

Lindsay's Principle of Continuity applies to both long-term intervals and the basic movements. It states that when one interval ends, the next begins immediately. A new basic movement or long-term interval is counted from the terminus of the previous basic movement or long-term interval. The only exception to that rule pertains to those basic movements which involve the rare sideways movement formation.

Principle of Alternation

The Principle of Alternation applies to the basic movements. It states that if the previous basic advance was long (or extended) then the basic advance currently underway will, in all likelihood, be short. If the previous basic advance was a short basic advance, then the current basic advance will, in all likelihood, be long or extended. The same principle is applicable to declines as well. The principle is not a perfect. It is more of a guideline than a rule. But it works often enough that it should be assumed true unless contradicted by a preponderance of the evidence. Review the alternation between short and long basic advances in Figure 2.2. The basic declines don't alternate nearly as orderly as the advances but, as Lindsay often wrote, declines don't conform to the guidelines nearly as well as advances.

Intervals of First Principle

"Intervals of First Principle" is the term I use to refer to two, very short intervals which occur throughout Lindsay's work. These intervals are the 107-day interval and 221-day interval. Both are point estimates which include surrounding windows of time. The 107-day interval is a time period which may extend from 102-112 days. Lindsay wrote that the 221-day interval is 221-225 days. This is the same time interval (7months and 10days) that Lindsay used in his <u>Three Peaks and a Domed House</u> model to time the high of a bull market. In my own work I have found that any interval from 215-225 days works well. Like the basic movements and long-term intervals, when these intervals coincide in time a turn in the market is the most likely outcome. These intervals are sometimes referred to as short-term counts.

Secondary Lows

The concept of a secondary low is not used to time the low itself; rather it is used to time the basic advance following the low. No matter how long a bear market lasts, there is usually an obvious low 13 to 14 months after the previous bull market high. Any remaining decline to a lower low, from the top of a bounce off of the 13/14 month low, has always been brief. A maximum decline of 101 days after the top of the bounce should be expected (assuming the ultimate low lies after the 13/14 month low and not before it). This 13-14 month low is an important low even though it may not be the ultimate low of the bear market. 13 to 14 months is the time span of a long basic decline. Per the Principle of Continuity the next basic advance must be counted from this low regardless of whether or not it is the ultimate low of the bear market. Sometimes this low comes prior to the ultimate low and sometimes it comes after. These lows are called Secondary Lows. A basic advance counted from a secondary low prior to the ultimate low is likely to be a long basic advance.

In Figure 5.7 a bull market ended on November 3, 1919. The bottom of the following bear market didn't appear until August 24, 1921. However, 14 months after the November high a temporary bottom, a secondary low, was printed on December 21, 1920. That bottom was 414 days, a long basic decline, from the high of the previous November. The Principle of Continuity directs us to count the next basic advance from this low.

The search for the bull market top of March 20, 1923 begins with a 15year interval. The March top is 15years, 4months from an important low on November 15, 1907. It is also 819 days, a long basic advance (742-830 days), from the secondary low of December 21, 1920. A long basic advance fits Lindsay's Principle of Alternation as the previous basic advance, from December 19, 1917 until November 3, 1919, was a short basic advance of 684 days.

After the high in March 1923 a 12year interval worked to pull the index down into a low. The high in June 1911 counts 12years, 5months to the low of October 27, 1923. The October low is an exact 221 days after the earlier high in March. The Dow experienced a steep bounce from that low but had not passed the 13/14month period yet. After topping in February 1924 the Dow turned back down into a secondary low on May 20, 1924. This low was 14 months, or 427 days (a long basic decline), from the high in March 1923 and functions as a secondary low. It was 12years, 11months from the June 1911 high which is somewhat long-in-the-tooth for a 12year interval. Perhaps that is why it was unable to breach the October 1923 low.

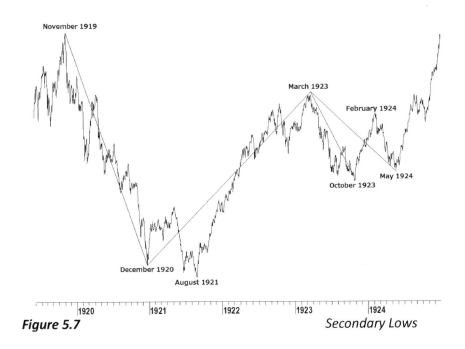

Figure 5.7   *Secondary Lows*

Sideways Movements

This concept explains how Lindsay dealt with those rare instances when he was unable to make a basic advance line up with a 15year interval. This situation is characterized by a scenario in which a basic advance cannot be stretched any longer, nor counted from any later date, and yet still does not reach the time-window of the earliest possible 15year interval (15years, 0months). Lindsay described this intervening time period between the end of a basic advance and the beginning of a 15year interval as a neutral period of time when the trend is theoretically neither up nor down. During this period of time, the overall result of price movement is approximately sideways regardless of what price may do in the interim. Lindsay sometimes referred to this as "extra time".

While bear markets are often characterized as V-shaped bottoms, bull market tops often play out as long, multi-month consolidations. Not all long consolidations are sideways movements, but when they are, Lindsay's short-term methods and middle section counts will target the final high of the long consolidation. That final high may, or may not, be the ultimate high but it will be one of the highs within the consolidation.

Eleven months has been the maximum duration of a sideways movement. The next basic decline is counted from the final high of the sideways movement (rather than from the end of the previous basic advance). This is the one exception to the Principle of Continuity. Alternatively, the 12year interval following a sideways movement is not necessarily counted from the final high; rather it is counted from the ultimate high of the movement. Lindsay wrote that, since 1842, he had identified 40 basic advances. Of those 40 basic advances only 5 were followed by sideways movements. Sideways movements occur infrequently.

The 1950's: A Case Study
Chapter 6

6. The 1950's: A Case Study

Before beginning a study of the decade following Lindsay's analysis in *"An Aid to Timing"* it is best to firm up Lindsay's "hunch" that a new long cycle had begun in 1942, rather than 1949, (chapter three, "The Old and New Alignments"). A confirmation of the basic cycles is made using middle section counts.

Middle Sections Counts and the Basic Cycles

Lindsay wrote that internal lows are found using the high of the final basic cycle in the previous long cycle as point J (Figure 6.1). If the long cycle terminated in 1942, then the high of the final basic cycle in the previous long cycle would have been the high of November 12, 1938.

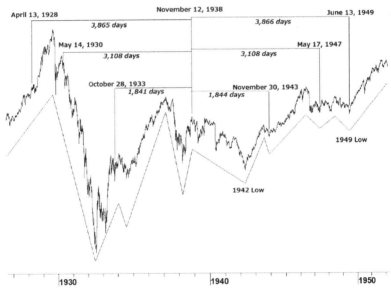

Figure 6.1   *Middle Section Counts*

The low on November 30, 1943 is 1,844 days past the high, point J, of November 12, 1938 (Figure 6.1). Point C on October 28, 1933, in a small ascending middle section that year, lies 1,841 days previous to point J. In addition, counting a 12year interval, from the beginning of the second basic decline in the 1929-1932 bear market (June 27, 1931), is 12years, 5months to the November 1943 low. This should be the bottom of the basic cycle that started on April 28, 1942. At only 139 days, it does not fit any of the standard time spans in its count from the July 14, 1943 high. Lindsay counted the basic decline to April 1944 (a subnormal basic decline of 285 days), a higher low than seen in 1943. It is a secondary low. The low on April 24, 1944 is followed by a long basic advance of 765 days to the high in May, 1946 (Figure 6.2).

The low of May 17, 1947 is 3,108 days after point J in November 1938. Exactly 3,108 days prior to that high, is point E of a descending middle section on May 14, 1930 (Figure 6.1). The low in May 1947 is 353 days (a short basic decline) from the bull market top on May 29, 1946 (Figure 6.2). It is also 12years, 3months after the high on February 18, 1935. This should be the end of a basic cycle from November 1943.

The low on June 13, 1949 is 3,866 days after point J in November 1938. April 13, 1928, the high of a flattened top, is 3,865 days prior to point J (Figure 6.1). The 1949 low is 12years, 3months from the March 10, 1937 high and is 364 days (a short basic decline) from the June 14, 1948 high (Figure 6.2). This low should be the bottom of a basic cycle from May 1947. It is also the end of the first multiple cycle which began in 1942.

Figure 6.2　　　　　　　　　　*Basic Movements 1942-1949*

The Decade Begins

As the bull market began in 1949, it could be seen that it would be interrupted by a 12year interval (counted from the August 14, 1937 top of a right shoulder) which would pull the Dow index down into a bottom (Figure 6.3). The higher, earlier high in March 1937 is associated with the low in June 1949. Assuming the standard 12years, 2months – 8months, the low would have been expected sometime between October 1949 and April 1950. Before a low could be made, however, a high would have to be printed.

Figure 6.3   *Long-term Intervals to 1950*

June 1950 High

22year Overlay: 1950

The 22year overlay told us not to expect a significant high in 1950 (Figure 6.4). While the 22, 15, and 8 year intervals fell seven years apart, none, but the eight-year interval, were of any significance. This was the first clue that the 12year low might not be the bottom of a basic cycle.

Figure 6.4   *22year Overlay, 1950 High*

Middle Section Counts

Point E (May 6, 1943) of the 1943 ascending middle section counts 1,296 days to the low of November 22, 1946. The high of June 12, 1950 arrives two days late, 1,298 days after the November 1946 low (Figure 6.5).

A count of 364 days from the high of June 14, 1948 to the low of June 13, 1949 is identical to the count between the June 13, 1949 low and the top on June 12, 1950 creating a mirror image in time. The June 1948 high is point E of a descending middle section stretching from the high of May 29, 1946 to the low of June 13, 1949 as the June 1949 low reaches a level that is lower than all the other lows between 1946 and 1949.

Figure 6.5   *June 1950 Middle Section Counts*

Counting from the bottom of the basic cycle at the June 1949 low, it was impossible to fit the time period to a high here into a standard time span. Even allowing for the top to be printed at the extreme end of the 15year interval (February 1951) would have been an advance of only 611 days; a subnormal basic advance. The time span between the June 1949 low and June 1950 high was only 364 days. This was not to be the end of a basic advance or the bull market.

July 1950 Low

Using a 15year interval, counted from the low of March 14, 1935, a high between March 1950 and February 1951 was expected. With the market not expected to top before March 1950 at the earliest, it was clear; the 12year low was going to be squeezed into its last few months. It was unknown, from just this information, that it would be three months past perfect (12years, 8months) and show up at the extreme of 12years and 11months past the 1937 high (Figure 6.3). The high of June 1950 was 15years and 3months from the low of March 1935.

The 12year low had to show up quickly as it was already beyond the typical limit of 12years, 8months. The market bottomed on July 13, 1950 only 31 days after the June high. The July low was 104 days after the March 31, 1950 low and within the +/- 5-day window of a 107-day interval (chapter five, Intervals of First Principle). As the long cycle was previously determined to have begun in 1942, the decade of the 1950s continued in the same long cycle. We would expect the interior lows (basic cycle lows) to still be counted to the same turning point (point J) on November 12, 1938.

The November high in 1938 is 4,261 days prior to the low in July 1950. Counting back an equidistance from the 1938 high targets a measuring point on March 14, 1927. This date is point E of a small descending middle section in February-March 1927. The low in 1950, while a 12year low (12years, 10months from the August 14, 1937 high) and successfully targeted using point J on November 12, 1938, is not the end of a basic decline. The advance from June 1949 to June 1950, at only 364 days, is too short for even a sub-normal basic advance (414-615 days) so the basic advance cannot be finished. Therefore, the July 1950 low cannot be the bottom of a basic cycle.

We can find other counts from middle sections to forecast the low in 1950. Counting from the low in July 1950 to the high on July 24, 1947 is 1,085 days. A descending middle section exists in July/August 1944. Point E on August 2, 1944 (the last day of the "line") is 1,086 days before the 1947 high (Figure 6.6). In addition, a short ascending middle section appears between April and June, 1950. Point E on May 11 counts 32 days to the June 12 high. The July low is 31 days later.

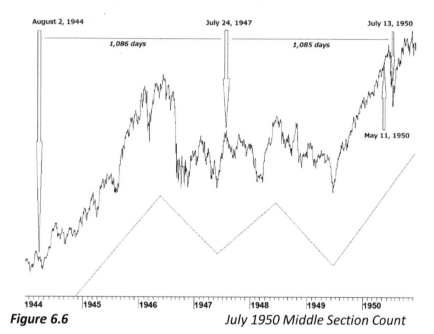

Figure 6.6   *July 1950 Middle Section Count*

June 1951 Low

After the peak in August 1937 which counted a 12year interval to the July 1950 low, the next obvious peak from which to count a 12year interval was in November 1938. The 12year interval from there pulled the Dow down into a low, 12years and 7months later, on June 29, 1951 (Figure 6.7). Like the low in 1950, it was nothing more than an interruption in the bull market and was timed using a descending middle section between June and November, 1943. Point E on August 18, 1943 counts 1,436 days to the high on July 24, 1947. The low in June 1951 is exactly 1,436 days after the July 1947 high.

Figure 6.7   *12year Intervals and Middle Section 1950-1951*

September 1951 High

After the low in July 1950 the search for the end of the ensuing advance begins.

22year Overlay: 1951

The 22-year overlay had a good fit with lows appropriately spaced seven years apart. It pointed to a high in 1951 (Figure 6.8). The lows, however, were not significant and told us not to expect a significant high in 1951.

Figure 6.8   *22year Overlay, 1951 High*

Interval Counts

The 15year interval is counted from the next significant low after the low in March 1935. That would be April 29, 1936. It targeted a top in the market between April 29, 1951 (15years, 0months) and March 1952 (15years, 11months) (Figure 6.9).

As the previous basic advance, ending in June 1948, had been short, the Principle of Alternation tells us to expect the current advance, from June 13, 1949, to be either long (742-830 days) or extended (929-968 days). A long basic advance would expire between June 25, 1951 and September 21, 1951. The interval narrows the time frame targeted by the 15year interval from 11months to 3months.

If the advance was to become extended, it would be expected to last until the period from December 29, 1951 until February 6, 1952. Again, these dates fit the 15year interval counted from April 1936. So the time frame to expect a high is found between June 25, 1951 and February 6, 1952 (Figure 6.9). We also need to exclude the period between the two standard time spans. That period is from September 22, 1951 (831 days) until December 28, 1951 (928 days).

Figure 6.9   *15year Interval , Basic Advance to September 1951 High*

Middle Section Counts

The high day of a flattened top falls on April 14, 1951 and counts 77 days to the low on June 29, 1951. The high on September 13, 1951 is 76 days later (Figure 6.10).

During the decline of 1948-1949 a small middle section formed with point E on May 4, 1949. Point E is 435 days before the low of July 13, 1950. The high on September 13, 1951 is 427 days later.

In table 4, the final middle section lists point C on March 7, 1947. That date counts 829 days to the low on June 13, 1949. The high on September 13, 1951 is 822 days later.

The high in September 1951 was a long basic advance of 822 days from the low of June 13, 1949.

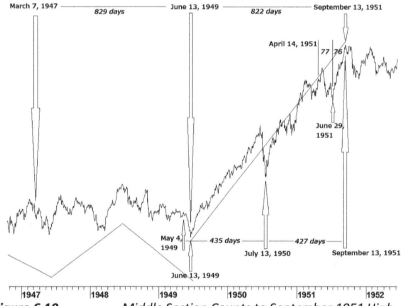

Figure 6.10   *Middle Section Counts to September 1951 High*

At this point it would have appeared we had targeted the end of the basic advance which began on June 13, 1949. The Dow never did make a new high between the high on September 13, 1951 and the final possible date of an extended basic advance on February 6, 1952.

May 1952 Low

The next peak after November 1938 was on September 12, 1939 and forecast a low between November 1951 (12years, 2months) and May 1952 (12years, 8months). Interior bear market lows are counted to the high of the final basic cycle in the previous long cycle (November 12, 1938). Using the high in November 1938 as point J, no middle section counts to this time period. Therefore, the May low in 1952 would not be considered the low of the basic cycle (Figure 6.11).

If we use the high on June 14, 1948 as point J, then the same descending middle section that was used to find the low in July 1950 counts 1,412 days from point E (August 2, 1944) to the June 1948 high. The low on May 1, 1952 is 1,417 days later. The low on May 1, 1952 managed to hold above the low in November 1951, albeit by less than one point, thus totally eliminating it from consideration as the low of the basic cycle from September 1949.

The low on May 1, 1952 is 220 days from the low on September 24, 1951 (Figure 6.11) which falls between the double top in September/October 1951 (chapter five, Intervals of First Principle).

Allowing for a decline from the top in September 1951 until the extreme end of the 12year interval (May 12, 1952) was only 242 days, a subnormal basic decline.

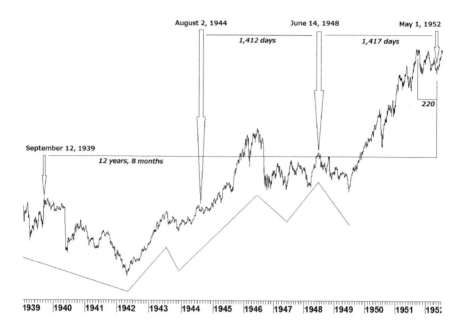

Figure 6.11   *12year interval, Middle Section Counts to May 1952 Low*

January 1953 High

Three Peaks and a Domed House

Once the advance re-ignited after the May 1, 1952 low (with that low never having breached the low in 1951) three peaks would have been apparent at the highs of September 1951, January 1952, and March 1952 (Figure 6.12). With the September and March highs being 6 ½ months apart, the model's requirement of peaks one and three being between six and ten months apart was fulfilled.

Another requirement of the model is for the low of the separating decline (the May 1, 1952) to reach a level lower than either one, or both, of the reactions following peaks one and/or two. This requirement was fulfilled when the May low breached the low on February 20, 1952 (the reaction following peak two).

Following the separating decline, a base consisting of two tests of the low (of the separating decline) must be identified. Those 'tests' were on May 16 and June 3, 1952. The base in 1952 was of the ascending variety which calls for a short domed house.

After the second test, a near-vertical move began (typical of the pattern) and is called the First Floor Wall. This ended on August 11, 1952 when the First Floor Roof began. In this case, rather than extending horizontally, the roof descended. This is seen in roughly half of all roofs throughout the history of the Dow index. More important than its direction, however, is the number of reversals contained within the roof. It contained the expected five reversals. They are identified with roman numerals in Figure 6.12. Once the fifth reversal bottomed in October, 1952, it was followed by another vertical move up until the top of the pattern on January 5, 1953.

Typically, a count of 221-224 days is made from the second test of the base to the top of the bull market. The ascending base told us to expect a short domed house and that usually requires making the count from earlier in the pattern. In this case 216 days transpired between the low in June 1952 and the bull market top in January 1953. This was the top of the basic cycle. The market then began a decline which did not end until September 1953 when the Dow reached the bottom of the pattern (bottom of the separating decline) as prescribed by Lindsay.

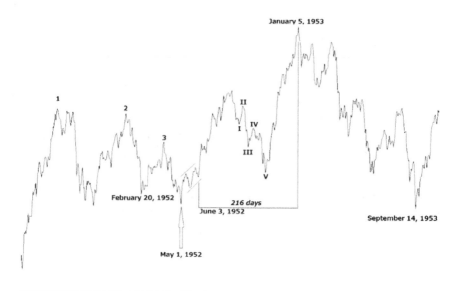

Figure 6.12   *Three Peaks and a Domed House, 1953 High*

The <u>Three Peaks and a Domed House</u> model is explained, in detail, in an educational DVD by the same name available at SeattleTechnicalAdvisors.com. The peak in 1953 can alternatively be interpreted as a hybrid form of the Three Peaks/Domed House model called 'Model 3' which is explained in the DVD.

Middle Section Counts

In Table 2, Lindsay shows point C of a descending middle section on September 25, 1941. That measuring point counts 2,060 days to the low on May 17, 1947. The high on January 5, 1953 is exactly 2,060 days later (Figure 6.13).

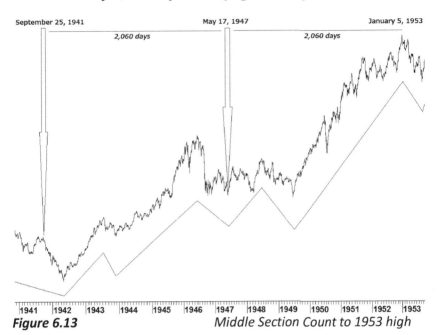

Figure 6.13   Middle Section Count to 1953 high

22year Overlay: 1953

The next 15year interval is counted from the low of March 31, 1938. In this case, again we find the lows separated by seven years but, apart from the 15year interval, none are significant and give no reason to expect a significant top (Figure 6.14). The 15year interval in 1938 was undercut by a lower low in 1942. This implies an interval closer to sixteen years than fifteen, but that wasn't to be the case this time.

June 23, 1930   March 31, 1938   July 27, 1945   January 5, 1953

29 30 31 32 33 34 35 36 37 38 39 40 41 42 43 44 45 46 47 48 49 50 51 52 53 54

Figure 6.14   *22year Overlay, 1953 High*

September 1953 Low

The high in September 1939 was used to forecast the 12year interval which terminated 12years and 8months later in May 1952. The next obvious high from which to count a 12year interval was on November 9, 1940. It forecast a low between January 1953 (12years, 2months) and July 1953 (12years, 8months). That time span overlapped with the12 year interval counted from September 1939 and may have been partly responsible for the May 1952 low.

The next candidate from which to count a 12year interval fell on July 28, 1941 (Figure 6.15). Lindsay's Principle of Continuity (chapter five) made this a likely candidate as it was the end of a 15year interval (15years, 4months) counted from the low of the sideways movement in 1926. The July 1941 high forecast a low in the time period September 1953 (12years, 2months) and March 1954 (12years, 8months).

Whether we assume the long cycle ended in either 1942 or 1949, counting from either of the highs of the final basic cycles (November 12, 1938 or June 14, 1948) did not produce counts which forecast the low on September 14, 1953 (the low of the Domed House). However, in Table 2 Lindsay shows a descending middle section with point E (last day of a line) on February 16, 1939. This measuring point is 2,659 days before the high of May 29, 1946 (coincidentally, the high of the multiple cycle that ended in 1949). The low of September 14, 1953 is 2,665 days after May 29, 1946 (Figure 6.15).

Despite not being able to use a middle section count from November 1938, the 1953 low is 252 days after the high on January 5, 1953, a subnormal basic decline, and more importantly, the end of a Three Peaks/Domed House pattern. We can safely conclude that it is the low of the basic cycle from 1949. It is from here that the next basic advance is to be counted.

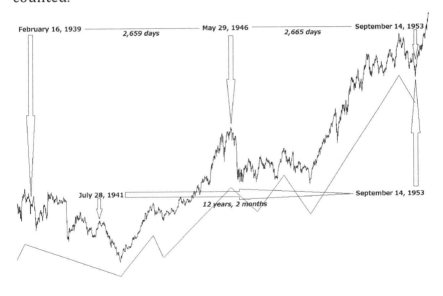

Figure 6.15　　　　*12year interval, Middle Section Count to 1953 Low*

August 1956 High

Interval Counts

After the low in March 1938 (the origin of the 15year interval which forecast the high in 1953) the next significant low (and the bottom of a basic cycle) did not appear until April 28, 1942. It forecast a high between April 1957 (15years, 0months) and March 1958 (15years, 11months). Counting a basic advance from the low of the basic cycle on September 14, 1953 it is quickly seen that the longest possible extended basic advance (968 days to May 9, 1956) will not reach to the earliest possible time for a 15year interval to expire in April 1957 (Figure 6.16). An earlier origin for the 15year interval is needed.

A low of some significance (but seemingly not as important as the low in April 1942) occurred on May 1, 1941. The shortest likely 15year interval (15years, 0months) would end in May 1956.

The 1953-56 bull market ended with a double-top in April and August, 1956 (Figure 6.16). The April high was 935 days from the low in 1953. That made it an extended basic advance (929 – 968 days) but the 15year interval forecast did not call for a top until one month later. The second top, on August 2, 1956, was 1,053 days after the low in 1953 and too long for any of the standard time spans. The period between April and August is a sideways movement.

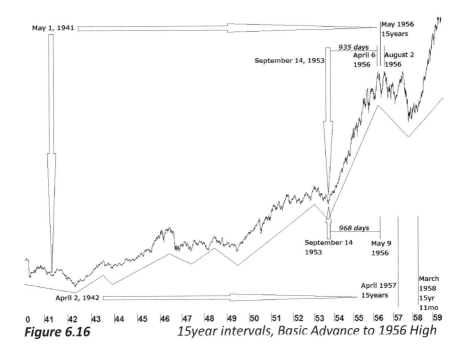

Figure 6.16   *15year intervals, Basic Advance to 1956 High*

In a newsletter written in 1972, Lindsay identified the time period in 1956, between April and August, as a sideways movement. A sideways movement is a period of time during which the overall result of price movement is approximately sideways (chapter five). A sideways movement starts with a sharp break followed by a recovery back to the approximate level of the old high. Eleven months is the maximum duration of the movement.

22 year overlay: 1956

The 22 year overlay was able to fit at lows but none of the lows was of any significance (Figure 6.17). The 15year low in May 1941 was breached a year later and was a hint that the interval would be extended to 16 years and the high might come in 1957, rather than 1956.

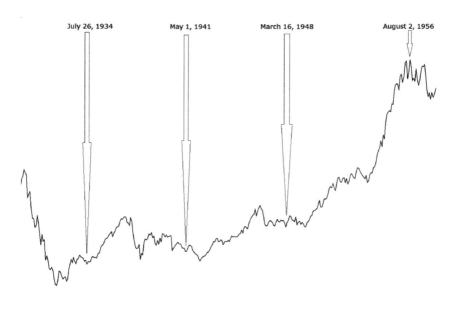

Figure 6.17   *22 year Overlay, 1956 High*

Middle Section Counts

Point C on February 19, 1951 counts 938 days to the low of the basic cycle on September 14, 1953 (Figure 6.18). The high on April 6, 1956 is 935 days past this turning point in 1953. This forecast for an end to the 1953 advance makes the basic advance 935 days and fits the time span of an extended basic advance (929-968 days). But it comes up short, by one month, of the 15year interval from May 1, 1941.

In October/November 1950 a descending middle section developed with point E on October 27, 1950. This measuring point counts 1,053 days to the same turning point on September 14, 1953. Counting forward another 1,053 days precisely forecasts the high of August 2, 1956. At 15years, 3months, this date is a better fit with the 15year interval from May 1, 1941. The time period between the end of the extended basic advance (April 6, 1956) and the high forecast by the second middle section (which matches the 15year interval) on August 2, 1956 is a sideways movement.

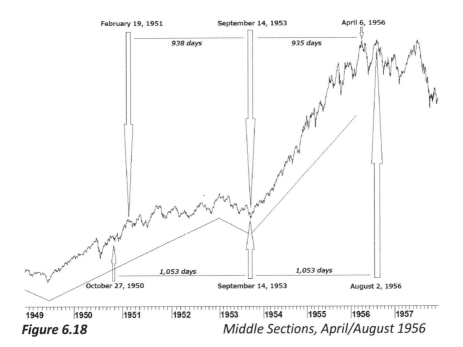

Figure 6.18   *Middle Sections, April/August 1956*

February 1957 Low

With the highs of 1956 having passed and a 15 year interval from April 1942 due to expire as soon as April 1957, an intervening low was expected. A 12 year interval from July 1941 had pulled the Dow down into the low of September 1953. The next high of any significance from which to count a 12year interval from was in July 1943. That high counted to a possible low between September 1955 and March 1956 but it expired before the sideways movement began in April. The next possible high from which to count a 12year interval was in July 1944. It forecast a low between September 1956 and March 1957. This time period was after the sideways movement and before the time period of a top forecast by the 15 year interval from April 1942 (April 1957 – March 1958).

In the bear market of 1953, point E of the final descending middle section occurred on July 7. It was 658 days before the high on April 26, 1955. 658 days later was the low of February 12, 1957.

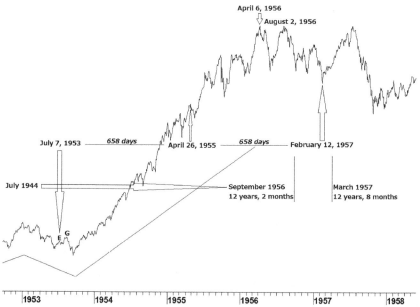

Figure 6.19   *12year interval, Middle Section Counts to 1957 Low*

July 1957 High

22year Overlay: 1957

The lows of April 28, 1942 and June 13, 1949 fit very nicely as 15 year and 8 year intervals (Figure 6.20). They called for a top in 1957. When two important counts so nearly coincide, the outcome is highly probable and a moderate decline did get underway on July 12, 1957. But with no important low 22 years prior to 1957 (the 1932 low was 25 years prior) the sell-off was destined to be "mild". The total loss was about 20%.

Figure 6.20   *22year Overlay, 1957 High*

Interval Counts and Middle Sections

After the low in February 1957, we need a point forecast for a top which matches the 15 year interval from April 1942 that tells us to expect a high between April 1957 and March 1958.

Although not a middle section count, taking a count from the high on July 14, 1943 to the low on July 13, 1950 is 2,556 days. Counting forward from July 13, 1950 to the high on July 12,

1957 is exactly 2,556 days creating a fascinating mirror image in time (Figure 6.21).

Point E on February 17, 1947 in a small descending middle section that year counts 1,900 days to May 1, 1952. Counting from this turning point in May 1952 to the high in July 1957 is 1,898 days.

The low of November 28, 1956 counts 226 days to the high in July 1957 (chapter five, Intervals of First Principle).

Figure 6.21   *15year Interval, Middle Section Counts to 1957 High*

October 1957 Low

The next significant high after the 'less-than-significant' high in July 1944 (used to count the 12 year interval to the low in February 1957) is not until May 29, 1946. A 12 year interval counted from this high forecasts a low between July 1958 (12 years, 2 months) and January 1959 (12years, 8months).

Lindsay prescribed that a basic decline should be counted from the final high in a sideways movement. In this case, that was August 2, 1956.

The longest possible long basic decline (446 days) only stretches until October 1957 forcing us to search for an earlier origin for a 12 year interval.

Exactly one year earlier, the high on May 29, 1945 forecasts a 12 year low between July 1957 and January 1958 (Figure 6.22).

The market unfolded in a long descending middle section between November 1938 and April 1939. In February 1939 the Dow index created a line with highs on February 4, 8, and 16. Counting from the first high in the line on February 4 to the high on June 14, 1948 is 3,418 days. Counting forward to the low on October 22, 1957 is 3,417 days.

The basic decline, counted from the final high of the sideways movement on August 2, 1956, counts 446 days to the low on October 22, 1957. 446 days is the longest possible long basic decline (376 – 446 days).

Figure 6.22   *12year Interval, Middle Section Counts to 1957 Low*

August 1959 High

22 year Overlay: 1959

The 22 year overlay gave a decent fit at market lows spaced the appropriate distance apart but none were significant lows (Figure 6.23). This indicated that the 'Moment of Truth' would not precede a significant pullback.

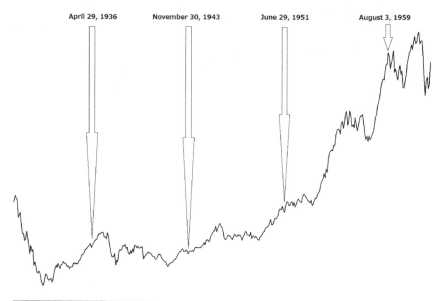

Figure 6.23   *22 year Overlay, 1959 High*

Interval Counts

With the rally into the high of April 1956 having been an extended basic advance (929-968 days), the Principle of Alternation would have us expecting a short basic advance (630 – 718 days) off the October low in 1957. An advance of this duration forecasts a high in the time period between July 14, 1959 and October 10, 1959. The advance into the high on August 3, 1959 lasted 650 days (Figure 6.24).

The next obvious low from which to count a 15year interval was on November 30, 1943. It forecast a high in the time period between November 1958 (15years) and October 1959 (15years, 11months). This 15year interval fits with a short basic advance off the low in 1957 (Figure 6.24).

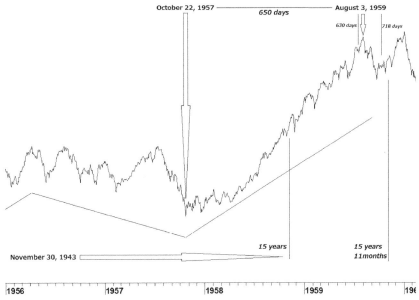

Figure 6.24   *15year Interval, Basic Advance to 1959 high*

Middle Section Counts

It's difficult to find a middle section which counts to this high. That fact, combined with the information derived from the 22 year overlay, would have us expecting only a short interruption in the uptrend despite our expectation for an end to the basic advance. The Dow dropped 10% into the September 1959 low.

September 1959 Low

Before the high in 1960 could be reached, the decline following the August high in 1959 would have to find a bottom. A 12year interval from February 1947 pulled the Dow index into a low 12 years and 7 months later on September 22, 1959 (Figure 6.25). This long-term interval had forecast a bottom between April 1959 (12 years, 2 months) and October 1959 (12 years, 8 months). A long-term interval counted from the high of July 24, 1947 probably played a role in pulling down the equity index as well. It counts 12 years and 2 months to the 1959 low.

The September low counts 105 days from the low on June 9, 1959 and 225 days from the low on February 9, 1959 (chapter five, Intervals of First Principle).

Using June 14, 1948 (4,117 days earlier) as the turning point, should take the count to a descending middle section. Instead, the count goes to Sunday, March 7, 1937; three days from the bull market top on March 10 of that year. Again, a mirror image in time is seen. No middle section counts to this low which tells us it is not the low of the basic cycle.

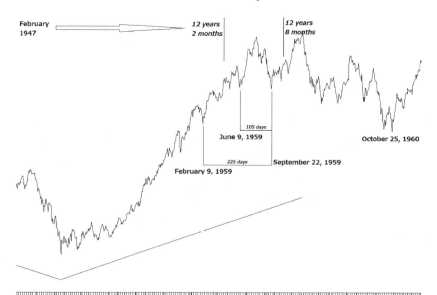

Figure 6.25   *12year Interval, Interval Counts to 1959 Low*

January 1960 High

Interval Counts

The 15 year interval, counted from April 1944 (Figure 6.26), forecast a market high in the period between April 1959 (15years) and March 1960 (15years, 11months). Another 15year interval from September 14, 1944 counts to a high in the period between September 1959 (15years) and August 1960 (15years, 11months). When intervals overlap like these two do, it is often the case that the eventual high in the Dow falls into the time period which belongs to both intervals; in this case that forecast time period would be narrowed to September 1959 – March 1960.

The high in 1960 was a higher high than seen previously in August 1959. The August high was the end of a short basic advance from October 1957. The high in 1960 is 805 days from the low in October 1957; a long basic advance. The Principle of Alternation had led us to expect a short basic advance because the rally into the April 1956 high had been extended. This is an example of why the Principle is treated as a guideline and not a rule. The answer to which date was to be the ultimate high is found in a count from a middle section.

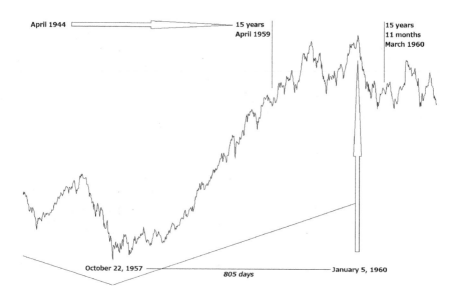

Figure 6.26   *15year Interval, Basic Advance to 1960 High*

Middle Section Count

A large ascending middle section unfolded between March 20, 1923 (point B) and March 30, 1926 point H). In Table 3, Lindsay lists point E as August 20, 1924. Point E counts 6,460 days to the low of the long cycle on April 28, 1942 (Figure 6.27). The high on January 5, 1960 occurred 6,461 days after that turning point. A forecast covering 36 years and off by only one-day!

In addition, a small ascending middle section appears between August and October, 1934 (not shown). Point E appears on September 27 and counts 4,615 days to a low on May 17, 1947. The high in January 1960 was printed 4,616 days later.

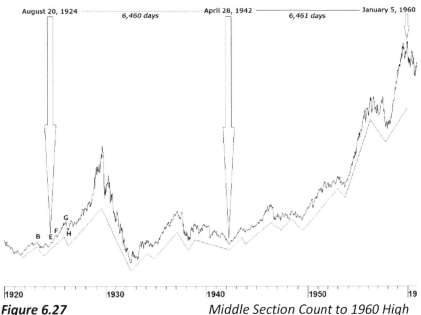

Figure 6.27   *Middle Section Count to 1960 High*

22year Overlay: 1960

The 22 year overlay was clear that the sell-off expected after the high in January 1960 would not be momentous (Figure 6.28). The bear market of 1960 gave up just less than 20% before hitting a low in October that year.

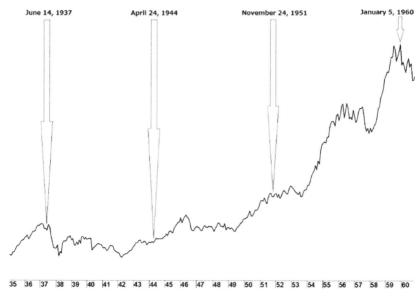

Figure 6.28   *22 year overlay, 1960 High*

October 1960 Low

Interval Counts

The high on June 14, 1948 (Figure 6.29) forecast a 12 year low between August 1960 (12 years, 2 months) and February 1961 (12 years, 8 months).

The previous basic decline into the October 1957 low, at 446 days, was the longest possible long basic decline. The Principle of Alternation leads to us to expect a short basic decline (or subnormal decline) from the high in 1960. The longest possible short basic decline (317 – 364 days) would see a bottom no later than January 3, 1961. The shortest possible short basic advance (317 days) meant the bottom would probably not come before November 17, 1960. In the end, the decline was a subnormal basic decline of 294 days to the low on October 25, 1960 and was timed by a middle section count.

Middle Section Counts

An ascending middle section is apparent between March and June 1959. Point C on March 16 counts 295 days to the high in January 1960. The final low on October 25, 1960 is 294 days later, a subnormal basic decline (Figure 6.29). Using the January high as a turning point would have us scratching our head wondering if the October low in 1960 was just the low of the basic cycle, or also the low of the long cycle from 1942.

If the low in April 1942 is the end of the previous long cycle (and not 1949), then an interior low in the current multiple cycle would count to November 12, 1938 (the high day of the final basic cycle of the previous long cycle) as a turning point. The October 1960 low counts 8,018 days to the November 1938 high. December 12, 1916 is point C of a descending middle section that year. It counts 8,005 days to the turning point in November 1938.

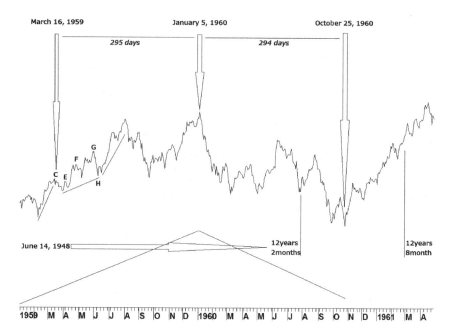

Figure 6.29   *12year Interval, Middle Section Count to 1960 Low*

In Tables 1, 2, and 3, Lindsay listed February 19, 1936 as point E of a small ascending middle section that year. Using June 14, 1948 as a turning point (assuming the long cycle ended in 1949), the two dates are 4,499 days apart. Counting forward from the turning point in 1948 the low on October 25, 1960 is 4,516 days later. If correct, this would have us thinking 1949 was the end of the long cycle. Without the benefit of previous examples, both of the above counts are close enough to leave one uncertain whether 1942 or 1949 was the end of the long cycle.

December 1961 High

Three Peaks and a Domed House

By the time the low in October 1960 was printed a Three Peaks pattern had emerged. Peak one was on August 3, 1959, peak two on January 5, 1960, and peak three on June 9, 1960 (Figure 6.30). Peaks one and three were the maximum ten months apart allowed by Lindsay.

Once the separating decline had reached its low in October 1960 it had breached both reaction lows following peaks one and two. The descending base told us to expect a long domed house; the typical 221-day count to the top of the bull market could not be counted from the base. In the case of a long domed house the count is normally taken from an inflection point in the First Floor Roof (5-wave reversal).

The five-wave reversal (roman numerals) between May 19 and July 12, 1961 has a fairly typical look about it. Descending roofs are seen in roughly half of all domed houses in the twentieth-century. Counting from the beginning of the reversals on May 19, 1961 counts only 208 days to the top of the bull market later that year in December. However, a count of 223 days forecasts the high of the right shoulder on December 28, 1961. It was from this point that the sell-off began in earnest.

As prescribed by Lindsay, the bear market following the December high did not stop until the Dow reached the bottom of the pattern. In this case it breached the low in October 1960 to see a 37% loss in the Dow.

Note how the ascending middle section in 1959 formed a 5-wave reversal in the advance into peak one which included a head-and-shoulders top; a fractal of a domed house.

Figure 6.30   *Three Peaks and a Domed House 1961*

Interval Counts

A 15year interval from the low of October 1946 forecast a high
sometime during the time period of October 1961 (15years)
and September 1962 (15years, 11months). Lindsay made clear
that the greatest probability of a high within this 11 month
time frame is 15years, 2months to 15years, 4months. This
narrow window targeted a high between December 1961 and
February 1962 (Figure 6.31). The high on December 13, 1961
made the interval 15years and 2months.

The decline into the October 1960 low had been subnormal so
the Principle of Alternation would have one expecting a long
basic decline (376-446 days) from the December 1961 high.
The 1961 top needed to be printed in time to squeeze in, at the
very least, a 376 day decline before the next bear market low. A
376 day decline counted backward from the latest likely date
(12years, 8months interval) on February 12, 1963 meant the
high needed to be printed no later than February 1, 1962.

Counting back 446 days from August 12, 1962 (12years, 2months), to find the earliest possible high, points to a top no earlier than May 23, 1961 but we already know the 15year interval doesn't call for a top until October 1961 at the earliest. This would have us looking for a top between October 1961 and February 1962.

The high in January 1960 followed a long basic advance (742-830 days) of 805 days. The Principle of Alternation expects the current advance, from the low on October 25, 1960, to be short (630-718 days) or subnormal (414-615 days). The shortest possible short basic advance (630 days) would have the bull market last until July 1962. Despite the problems counting to a high using the Three Peaks/Domed House pattern, it was clear that July 1962 would make the domed house far too long as well as not fit the targets determined above. A subnormal basic advance targeted the time period between December 13, 1961 and July 2, 1962. The high of the bull market (and domed house) was on December 13, 1961 (Figure 6.31). This was one of the very few sub-normal basic advances in history.

Figure 6.31   *15year Interval and Basic Advance to 1961 High*

221

Middle Section Counts

The intra-day high of the bull market occurred, not in December, but a month earlier on November 15, 1961. Lindsay was clear that middle sections are counted to the dates of intra-day highs and lows.

In Table 2 Lindsay lists October 23, 1922 as point C in a large ascending middle section which lasts until October 1923. It counts 7,127 days to the low of the long cycle on April 28, 1942. A time span of 7,141 days extends from the bottom of the long cycle to the high on November 15, 1961 (Figure 6.32). A miss of 14 days over a forecast of 39 years! It is this middle section count which leads us to believe that the high in November 1961 was not only the end of the short bull market from October 1960, but the final high in the multiple cycle from 1942.

October 5, 1959 is point E of a small ascending middle section from late September to late October that year. It counts 386 days to the low on October 25, 1960. Counting forward another 386 days arrives at the intraday high of the bull market on November 15, 1961 (Figure 6.32).

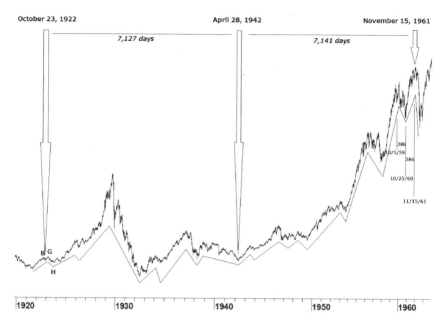

Figure 6.32   *Middle Section Counts to November 1961 High*

Other middle sections (not shown) pointing to the November high can be found as well...

A small ascending middle section occurs in September-October 1953. With only two rallies in the middle section, September 28, 1953 becomes point E and counts 1,485 days to the low on October 22, 1957. Counting forward another 1,485 days arrives at the bull market high on November 15, 1961.

July 10, 1945 is point E of a descending middle section during the summer of 1945. It counts 2,988 days to the low on September 14, 1953. The November 1961 high is 2,984 days later.

A small descending middle section formed in August-September 1959. Point E on August 21 counts 431days to the low on October 25, 1960. Another 431 days forward counts, not to the November 1961 high, but to the right shoulder on December 28, 429 days later.

22year Overlay: 1961

Important lows, 7 years apart, are spotted in October 1946 and September 1953 (Figure 6.33). Two important lows set apart as these two are indicate a top 15 and 8 years later, respectively, in 1961. But no important low exists 22 years prior to 1961 in 1939. A minor low in 1939 can be counted 22 years forward to the 1961 high but a major low is normally required for a bear market of the first magnitude. The forecast then was for a respectable pullback in 1961. The total loss that year was about 37%. A bad bear market, to be sure, but not one that met Lindsay's idea of significant.

October 9, 1946

September 14, 1953

December 13, 1961

|37 |38 |39 |40 |41 |42 |43 |44 |45 |46 |47 |48 |49 |50 |51 |52 |53 |54 |55 |56 |57 |58 |59 |60 |61 |62 |63

Figure 6.33   *22year Overlay, December 1961*

June 1962 Low

Interval Counts

After the high of June 1948 (used to forecast the October 1960 low) the next significant high was on June 12, 1950. It forecast a low in the time period between August 1962 (12years, 2months) and February 1963 (12years, 8months).

The decline into the October 1960 low, at 294days was a subnormal basic decline. Therefore the Principle of Alternation would have us expecting a long basic decline (376-446 days) to follow the high in 1961. This time frame is the period December 1962 – March 1963.

The ultimate low was on June 26, 1962 and long before the medium-term intervals listed above would have led us to expect it. In this case we would have found ourselves counting to a secondary low on October 23, 1962 which bottomed 4% above the June low earlier that year. Sometimes it is more accurate to use intraday figures than closing prices. Counting from the high on November 15, 1961 to the secondary low in October 1962 is 342 days, a short basic decline. The June low was 223 days from the high in November 1961 and 103 days from the high on March 15, 1962 (chapter five, Intervals of First Principle).

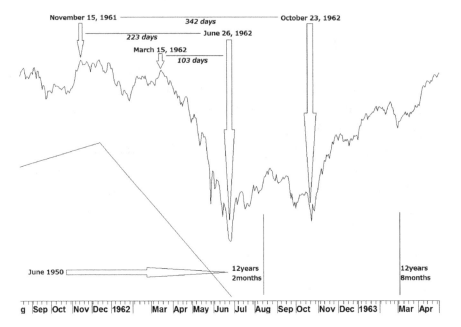

Figure 6.34   *Interval Counts to 1962 Lows*

Middle Section Counts

Point E on May 31, 1961 of a small descending middle section counts 196 days to the high on December 13, 1961. The low on June 26, 1962 is 195 days after the bull market high in December 1961 (Figure 6.35). It was noted previously that middle sections are counted to intra-day highs and lows, not closing prices. That implies the count should have gone to the November high. This is a good reminder that one should examine all the possibilities particularly when there are other confirming counts as in Figure 6.34.

Lindsay wrote that the low of a terminal bear market (the low of a long cycle) is counted to the high of the same multiple cycle. A middle section count to the high in 1961 would make the June 1962 low the end of the long cycle from 1942. Another clue that the low in 1962 was the end of the long cycle was that the decline from 1961 was the fourth decline during the 1949 multiple cycle stretching to the limit of what has been seen previously in history.

Lindsay often wrote of a concept, similar to a mirror image, called the Low-Low-High interval. It involved determining the time between two lows and then counting the same number of days forward in time expecting to find a high. It needed to forecast a date which matched forecasts from his other models, of course. In only one newsletter did he ever make mention of the opposite approach, a High-High-Low interval. In the search for the 1962 low it should be noted that counting from the high of July 12, 1957 to the high of January 5, 1960 is 907 days. Counting 907 days forward from the 1960 high misses the June 1962 low by only 4 days (Figure 6.35).

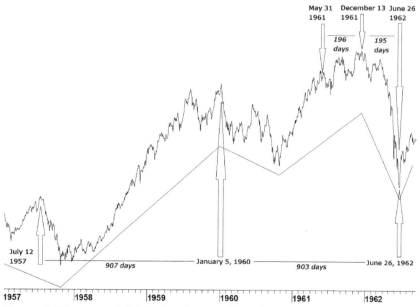

Figure 6.35   *Middle Section, High-High-Low Counts to 1962 Low*

ABOUT THE AUTHOR

Ed Carlson, author of the books *An Aid to Timing* and *George Lindsay and the Art of Technical Analysis*, is an independent trader, consultant, and Chartered Market Technician (CMT) based in Seattle, Washington. Carlson manages the website Seattle Technical Advisors.com, where he publishes daily and weekly commentary. He lectures across the US and Canada on the methods of George Lindsay. He spent twenty years as a stockbroker and holds an M.B.A. from Wichita State University.

Made in the USA
Middletown, DE
14 July 2022

69382861R00129